Baltimore's Mansion

National Bestseller
Winner of the Charles Taylor Prize for Literary Non-Fiction
Shortlisted for the 1999 Governor General's Award for Non-Fiction

"A love letter not only to [Johnston's] homeland, but to his father, a staunch anti-Confederate unable to relinquish his vision of what Newfoundland once was and could have been. Thanks to Johnston's powers of evocation, the reader is able to share a fleeting glimpse of that vision." —Lynn Coady, *Chatelaine*

"A humane and winning book, passionate and yet careful in its articulation of the old story of fathers and sons, poetic in its narrative freedom, but very personal as well." —*The Gazette* (Montreal)

"This is an absorbing, sometimes amusing, often moving read, carried strongly by Mr. Johnston's fine prose." —*Ottawa Citizen*

"A great companion to *The Colony of Unrequited Dreams*.... The family's political fury gives zip to Johnston's decision to write about Smallwood and both books reveal the frightening grandeur of the land."
—*The Hamilton Spectator*

"*Baltimore's Mansion* is an unusual and vibrant book, a fine tribute to the island that has been such a formidable part of the Johnston and other clans, a land whose influence is hard to define but is evident in the way one views the world." —*The Edmonton Journal*

"Deftly weaving family stories, political history and Arthurian legend, Johnston reflects on the tragic destiny of 'the Avalon', a community that once believed it could be an island—and a nation—unto itself."
—*Elm Street*

"Easily one of the best memoirs ever published in this country."
—*The Record* (Kitchener–Waterloo)

"[A] beautifully woven...collection of memories taken intact and replayed so clearly the reader becomes an intimate bystander. Long after the book is put down the images will continue to swirl within easy grasp." —*New Brunswick Telegraph Journal*

Also by Wayne Johnston

The Story of Bobby O'Malley
The Time of Their Lives
The Divine Ryans
Human Amusements
The Colony of Unrequited Dreams

Baltimore's Mansion

A   M e m o i r

Wayne Johnston

VINTAGE CANADA
A Division of Random House of Canada Limited

VINTAGE CANADA EDITION, 2000

Copyright © 1999 by 1310945 Ontario Inc.

Canadian Cataloguing in Publication Data

Johnston, Wayne, 1958–
    Baltimore's mansion : a memoir

ISBN 0-676-97297-7

1. Johnston, Wayne, 1958–   — Biography.   2. Johnston, Wayne, 1958–
— Family.   3. Fathers and sons — Newfoundland.   4. Newfoundland — Social life and customs.   5. Novelists, Canadian (English) — 20th century — Biography.   I. Title.

PS8569.O3918Z53 2000   C813'.54   C00-931353-2
PR9199.3.J599Z464 2000

Text design and maps: CS Richardson

Visit Random House of Canada Limited's Web site: www.randomhouse.ca

Printed and bound in the United States of America

10 9 8 7 6 5 4 3 2

For the Johnstons of Ferryland

For the Callanans—Laus, Cindy, Tim and Joey—of St.John's

"The Forge hath been finished this five weekes . . . wee have prospered to the admiration of all beholders. . . . All things succeed beyond my expectation."

From a letter by Captain Edward Wynne, Governor of the Colony of Ferryland, reporting on the progress of Baltimore's mansion, to the colony's patron, Lord Baltimore, who took residence in the spring of 1627.

Ferryland, July 28, 1622

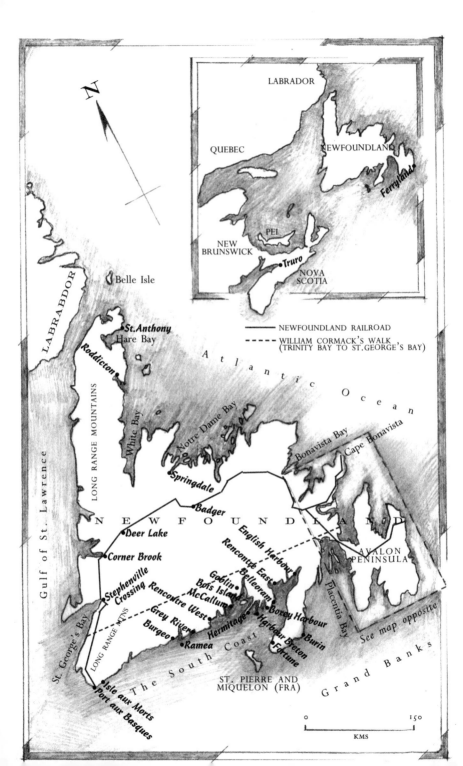

N

LABRADOR

QUEBEC

NEWFOUNDLAND

Ferryland

NEW
BRUNSWICK

PEI

NOVA
SCOTIA

•**Truro**

Belle Isle

LABRADOR

St.Anthony
Hare Bay

Roddicton

LONG RANGE MOUNTAINS

White Bay

Notre Dame Bay

A t l a n t i c   O c e a n

Bonavista Bay

Cape Bonavista

——— NEWFOUNDLAND RAILROAD
- - - - WILLIAM CORMACK'S WALK
(TRINITY BAY TO ST.GEORGE'S BAY)

Springdale

•**Badger**

N E W F O U N D L A N D

•**Deer Lake**

English Harbour

•**Corner Brook**

Rencontre East

AVALON
PENINSULA

Gulf of St. Lawrence

**Stephenville
Crossing**

Rencontre West

Goblin

Belleoram

Botts Island

McCallum

Boxey Harbour

Burin

LONG RANGE MTNS

Grey River

Hermitage

Harbour Breton

Placentia Bay

Burgeo

•**Ramea**

Fortune

See map opposite

St. George's Bay

T h e   S o u t h   C o a s t

ST. PIERRE AND
MIQUELON (FRA)

G r a n d   B a n k s

Isle aux Morts
Port aux Basques

0   150

KMS

I AM FOREBORN of spud runts who fled the famines of Ireland in the 1830s, not a man or woman among them more than five foot two, leaving behind a life of beggarment and setting sail for what since Malory were called the Happy Isles to take up unadvertised positions as servants in the underclass of Newfoundland.

Having worked off their indenture, they who had been sea-fearing farmers became seafaring fishermen and learned some truck-augmenting trade or craft that they practised during the part of the year or day when they could not fish.

Their names.

In reverse order: Johnston. Johnson. Jonson. Jenson... MacKeown. "Mac" in Gaelic meaning "son" and Keown "John."

MY FATHER GREW up in a house that was blessed with water from an iceberg. A picture of that iceberg hung on the walls in the front rooms of the many houses I grew up in. It was a blown-up photograph that yellowed gradually with age until we could barely make it out. My grandmother, Nan Johnston, said the proper name for the iceberg was Our Lady of the Fjords, but we called it the Virgin Berg.

In 1905, on June 24, the feast day of St. John the Baptist and the day in 1497 of John Cabot's landfall at Cape Bonavista and "discovery" of Newfoundland, an iceberg hundreds of feet high and bearing an undeniable likeness to the Blessed Virgin Mary appeared off St. John's harbour. As word of the apparition spread, thousands of people flocked to Signal Hill to get a glimpse of it. An ever-growing flotilla of fishing boats escorted it along the southern shore as it passed Petty Harbour, Bay Bulls, Tors Cove, Ferryland, where my father's grandparents and his father, Charlie, who was twelve, saw it from a rise of land known as the Gaze.

At first the islands blocked their view and all they could see was the profile of the Virgin. But when it cleared Bois

Island, they saw the iceberg whole. It resembled Mary in everything but colour. Mary's colours were blue and white, but the
Virgin Berg was uniformly white, a startling white in the sun-
light against the blue-green backdrop of the sea. Mary's cowl
and shawl and robes were all one colour, the same colour as
her face and hands, each feature distinguishable by shape alone.
Charlie imagined that, under the water, was the marble
pedestal, with its network of veins and cracks. Mary rode without one on the water and there did not extend outwards from
her base the usual lighter shade of sea-green sunken ice.

The ice was enfolded like layers of garment that bunched
about her feet. Long drapings of ice hung from her arms, which
were crossed below her neck, and her head was tilted down
as in statues to meet in love and modesty the gaze of suppli-
cants below.

Charlie's mother fell to her knees, and then his father
fell to his. Though he wanted to run up the hill to get a
better look at the Virgin as some friends of his were doing,
his parents made him kneel beside them. His mother reached
up and, putting her hand on his shoulder, pulled him down.
A convoy of full-masted schooners trailed out behind the iceberg like the tail of some massive kite. It was surrounded at
the base by smaller vessels, fishing boats, traps, skiffs, punts.
His mother said the Hail Mary over and over and blessed herself repeatedly, while his father stared as though witnessing
some end-of-the-world-heralding event, some sight foretold by
prophets in the last book of the Bible. Charlie was terrified
by the look on his father's face and had to fight back the urge
to cry. Everywhere, at staggered heights on the Gaze, people
knelt, some side-on to keep their balance, others to avert their

eyes, as if to look for too long on such a sight would be a sacrilege.

A man none of them knew climbed the hill frantically, lugging his camera, which he assembled with shaking hands, trying to balance the tripod, propping up one leg of it with stones. He crouched under his blanket and held above his head a periscope-like box which, with a flash and a puff of foul-smelling yellow smoke, exploded, the mechanism confounded by the Virgin, Charlie thought, until days later when he saw the picture in the *Daily News*. Even then it seemed to him that the Virgin must have lent the man's machine the power to re-create in black and white her image on the paper, the same way she had willed the elements to fashion her image out of ice.

He had seen photographs before but had never watched as one was taken. She was the first object he had seen both in real life and in photographs. For the rest of his life, whenever he saw a photograph, he thought of her and the man he had been so surprised to see emerge unharmed from beneath his blanket.

How relieved he was when the Virgin Berg and her attending fleet sailed out of sight and his parents and the other grownups stood up and blessed themselves. Soon the miracle became mere talk, less and less miraculous the more they tried to describe what they had seen, as if, now that it was out of sight, they doubted that its shape had been quite as perfect as it seemed when it was looming there in front of them.

They heard later of things they could not see from shore, of the water that ran in rivers from the Virgin, from her head and from her shoulders, and that spouted from wound-like punctures in her body, cascading down upon the boats below, onto the fishermen and into the barrels and buckets they manoeuvred into place as best they could. Some fishermen stood, eyes closed and mouths wide open, beneath the little waterfalls, gulping and gagging on the ice-cold water, their hats removed, their hair and clothing drenched, hands uplifted.

The priests and nuns were at the wharf when the ice-laden fishing boats returned, the boats riding low so weighted down were they with water and with ice fragments that had been salvaged from around the berg — leavings, chunks, bergy bits and growlers — that they had snared with gaffs and nets or had hacked off and dragged aboard. The water and ice were loaded into barrels donated by a merchant for the purpose, and the barrels were taken to the sacristy, then down to the basement where they were kept like casks of wine, consecrated by a bishop and afterwards used sparingly as holy water in the sacrament of Extreme Unction and, in rare cases, in baptisms and the blessings of houses.

My great-grandfather's house was blessed with water from the iceberg because he was a blacksmith. My father told me this as if it was self-evident why a blacksmith should be so honoured. Droplets of water thawed after ten thousand years, water in its liquid form for the first time in ten millennia, were splashed on the walls, floors and windows, on the chairs, the tables and the beds and on every part of Charlie's father's forge, the forge that the priest believed was for sacredness second only to the church.

Nan told my father when he was nine that she could see the stains where the water had been sprinkled thirty years ago. She pointed to places on the wall and on the floor. "See," she said, but no matter how closely my father stared at the flowered pattern in the wallpaper or at the linoleum on the kitchen floor, he could not see what she was pointing at.

There were two versions of the story of the ultimate fate of the Virgin Berg, and my father did not know which was true. In one version, the fishermen stayed with the iceberg until it floated southward, away from the island, out to sea. In the other version, it ran aground on the shoals of Cape St. Mary's and in some spectacular fashion was destroyed.

When I went to school, the nuns told us that the Virgin Berg started out from the glaciers of Greenland as an amorphous chunk of ice which the God-wielded elements gradually moulded into a statue of the Blessed Virgin Mary, the Berg slowly taking shape as it floated down past Baffin Island and the coast of Labrador until, when the sun rose on June 24, 1905, it appeared fully formed off the headlands of St. John's, a city named after the Baptist whose feast day this was. That June 24 was also the day of Cabot's discovery of Newfoundland left no question in the minds of Catholics that the iceberg was a sign in confirmation of the fact that God was one of them and a sign to Protestants of God's disfavour.

I thought of the Virgin Berg moving slowly southward in the dark of night on the Labrador current, by day too far from shore to be encountered by fishing boats, far from the shipping lanes, an unseen work-in-progress, its nine-times-as-large pedestal submerged, dredging trenches in the ocean floor, plowing through whatever it encountered.

Even in these daydreams, I could not decide how the Virgin Berg had met its end. I liked to think of it as it continued south, beyond the range of the fishing boats, disappearing slowly from view, that Virgin of ice regally erect. For how long, again unseen, had it persisted in the likeness of the Virgin? Probably not long, once it encountered the warm Gulf Stream.

Even more vividly I imagined the Virgin foundering on the shoals of Cape St. Mary's. Where else should an iceberg shaped like Mary meet its end? Great chunks of ice sliding off into the water, cracks appearing in the base until, in one grand explosion, it disintegrated from within, the Virgin's head falling first, toppling from the shoulders, then a chaos of ice and ocean, God's handiwork undone in a God-like, apocalyptic way.

For years, Ferryland existed for me only as the place from which the photograph was taken, a prospect off-camera from which the view of the Virgin Berg grew dimmer day by day. I did not know what it meant that my father was "from" this place. I wondered where he'd be from when there was nothing in the photograph but fog.

WHEN I WAS six, I believed what my parents and all my aunts and uncles wished were true, that the Avalon Peninsula, "the Avalon" we called it, was itself a country. It is joined to the main island of Newfoundland by an isthmus so narrow that, while standing in the middle of it, you can see the ocean from both sides. My father said we should dig a canal through the isthmus and declare our independence. He felt this way because of something darkly called "the referendum." I knew nothing more about it than its name. When I asked him, he said it meant, "We used to be a country, but we're not one any more."

The Avalon. The nuns told us that one of the first New World colonists, England's secretary of state, Lord Baltimore, called the colony he founded in the 1620s "Avalon" because of a legend according to which St. Joseph of Arimathea introduced Christianity to Britain in a place called Avalon in Somerset-shire. But they did not tell us how that first Avalon had got its name.

They did not tell us that in one of the Arthurian legends Avalon was the name of an island somewhere to the west of

England where King Arthur sailed to be healed of his wounds. I found this out by reading Malory's *Morte d'Arthur*, a copy of which was found among the possessions of Aunt Freda, my father's sister, who grew up in Ferryland, acquired a master of arts in English literature and died of cancer when she was forty-three.

There were many parallels between my world and the one portrayed in the book, parallels that Freda herself seemed to have noted, for there were little checkmarks in the margins. It so happened that my father's first name was Arthur and his second Reginald, which I was told meant "King." I'm sure these coincidences meant more to me than they did to Freda; but Freda — perhaps for personal reasons that I was too young to appreciate — had put a checkmark by what was to become my favourite part of *Morte d'Arthur*.

It was the part in which the dying King declares: ". . . I will into the vale of Avilion to heal me of my grievous wound; and if thou hear never more of me, then pray ye for my soul."

Then Sir Bedivere puts the wounded Arthur on board a barge "with many fair ladies in it, and among them all was a queen, and all they had black hoods, and all they wept and shrieked when they saw King Arthur."

The two images, the image of the Virgin Berg and that of the barge with its cargo of hooded queens, merged in my mind to form various hybrid images. I pictured an iceberg with not one but several massive statues, the hooded queens surrounding the Virgin who reared up above them. Sometimes there were just the hooded queens, human sized, and they appeared from out of the fog not on a wooden barge but on a pan of ice, as if they had been set adrift against their will. Sometimes on the pan of ice the hooded queen, unaccompanied by her attendants, stood with her arms folded on her breast in mimicry of the queen of heaven in the photograph.

An arrow pointed from the word "Avilion" to a note my aunt had written in the margin: "Avalon, the Celtic abode of the blessed. An island paradise in the western seas where King Arthur and the other heroes of the Arthurian legends went when they were dying. In one legend, the 'Isle of Apples' to which the dying Arthur was taken."

I understand now why the nuns traced the derivation of Avalon no further back than St. Joseph of Arimathea, for this Isle of Apples sounds very much like a pagan Garden of Eden. Another note in my aunt's book read: "Over the years, the legend of Avalon was modified and the location of Avalon was changed. By the thirteenth century, it was believed to be Glastonbury in Somerset, where, according to legend, Joseph of Arimathea, escaping from persecution in his homeland, built the first Christian church in England. So it was that Baltimore, a follower of the legend, chose 'Avalon' as the name for his Roman Catholic colony at Ferryland."

Poor Baltimore. He thought it was a heavenly haven he was going to when he set sail with his family in the late 1620s, a colony created at his command and now ready to receive him. But I did not think of him then as poor Baltimore but as Baltimore, "a follower of a legend," which it seemed to me was a great thing to be, no matter what the legend was, all the more so when it was that of Arthur and Avalon.

So there were two Avalons, the Avalon where we lived and the Avalon to which, like King Arthur, we would travel when we died.

Perhaps once a summer, for the first few summers after I

started school, we drove as far as the isthmus but never past it. It was almost always foggy there. Owing to the narrowness of that strip of land, the wind was onshore regardless of which way it was blowing, and fog was almost always racing across the isthmus from one direction or the other. It was a place of confluence, turbulence. It was for the same reason always cold there; at the narrowest point of the isthmus, a trench of glacial rubble like the long-dried-up bed of some ancient river ran from sea to sea, a trench strewn with boulders and jagged shards of granite. The rest was bedrock. Over it in some places was laid a mat of root-woven sod on which dwarf spruce and alders somehow grew, their roots like tentacles, enclosing rocks, four and five feet of them exposed between the mat of sod on the boulder and the ground beneath it into which the roots were sunk.

I could always tell when we were nearing the isthmus, for on sunny days it became foggy, and on foggy days so much more foggy that all the world except the inside of the car was blotted out. Although it was no more than a few miles deep, as soon as we drove into the fog we turned around, as if we could no more go farther than if the road had been washed out. We did not have any agreed-upon point of return, for the depth of that sea-spanning stream of fog varied.

The Isthmus of Avalon. The isthmus. It was the edge of the known world, and looked it. The word itself evoked the place. Or the place had inspired the word. Like the word, the isthmus seemed to have been fashioned out of mist, a sibilant, lisping mist, an "I" with "mist" on either side.

In *Morte d'Arthur* Avalon is the place of death. I knew that when Arthur said he was going to Avalon "to heal me of my grievous wound," he meant that he was going to a place beyond life, an afterlife, from which he would not return. But I did not think of him as having died or experienced "death" as that concept had been explained to me at school. Heaven, hell, purgatory, limbo, Arthur had not gone to one of these afterlives; he had gone to Avalon, where he was healed. I believed, inasmuch as I was able to think it through, that though we did not live in the mythical Avalon itself, we lived in a place thought by Baltimore to be so much like it, so favoured as to be worthy of bearing its name. In the same way, although I knew that my father was not Malory's King Arthur, I thought of him as a man whose name set him apart, Arthur Reginald, a King-like, Arthur-like man among mere knights or even lesser beings who had never been a child, a man who had simply "arrived" among us and, because of his Arthur-like qualities, had been given Arthur's name and title.

I had the vague notion that we turned around when we did so as not to cross over into the place where my father would receive a "grievous wound" and go from there to the mythical Avalon where, though healed, he would be apart from us. I thought that beyond the stream of fog lay not Avalon but another afterworld where the grievous wounds of people who had died remained unhealed, the Arthurian equivalent of hell or purgatory. It was, among other things, the lair of "the Baymen," a tribe by which, as I would soon be told, our independence was undone, an inscrutably sinister domain.

The rest of the island beyond the Avalon lay in outer darkness, beyond the uncrossable mist, unknown except in the lore of scorn, the place of the fearsomely dense people known as the baymen, who in the distant past had inflicted upon us a "grievous wound." It would be years before I understood the nature of that wound: on July 22, 1948, in a referendum ordered by Britain, in which the choices were independence or confederation with Canada, Newfoundlanders voted by the barest of margins for confederation. On the Avalon, the vote was two to one for independence, and outside the Avalon two to one for Canada. "Forgive them Lord, they know not what they did," my father said.

OUTWARD FROM FERRYLAND Avalon grew, without help from its founder, Lord Baltimore, who died in 1632, not long after spending his one and only winter there. The colonists that Baltimore sent ahead of him to build his mansion house had indeed built it, he was told when he arrived, but had otherwise done little else but pass the time in "idlenesse and debauchyre."

By January, he was sharing his mansion house with fifty scurvy-ridden colonists, ten of whom, though the accommodations were far superior to what they were accustomed to, perished.

He left Ferryland for good in the spring of 1629. The only thing of his that endured was the name he had chosen for his colony — Avalon, named after the birthplace of Christianity in England. He was a recent convert to Catholicism, and most of the settlers he took with him to the New World were Catholics.

A Protestant, the duke of Hamilton, David Kirke, was given a patent to the entire island of Newfoundland, including the province of Avalon, in 1637, but it became a Baltimore family tradition to litigate against this patent, which generation after generation did for at least a hundred years. It was considered one's family duty as a Baltimore to sue for the ownership of Avalon long after the last Baltimore who had set eyes on it was dead. The impossibly complicated and protracted litigation over Avalon makes the lawsuits in *Bleak House* seem expeditious by comparison. It is not known exactly when this legacy of litigation petered out. If an authoritative decision was ever rendered, no record of it remains.

Twenty years after leaving the place, my father still likened people he met, or saw on television, to people who were famous or notorious in Ferryland for something — miserliness, ugliness, short-sightedness. Those of any profession whom he judged to be inept — athletes, politicians, actors — he dismissed with the observation that "Paddy Haley would have done a better job."

None of us, not even my mother, knew who Paddy Haley was; nor did we know anything of Nell Hines, whom he judged a good many people to be "more miserable" than, meaning tight with money and generally joyless. If he wished to impress upon us how large a man he met or saw was, he would tell us he "swore to god" that "he was bigger than Howard Morrey," or had "a pair of hands on him twice the size of Howard Morrey's." I had no more idea than anyone who did not grow up in Ferryland when my father did what Howard Morrey's dimensions were.

Ferryland, though only forty miles south of where we lived on the outskirts of St. John's, seemed to me impossibly remote, much farther from home than the isthmus of Avalon, which was in fact twice as far away. Though I didn't realize it at the time, this was because the road to Ferryland followed the coastline, and for most of the trip we were mere feet from the sea, which we could not smell or even see from where we lived. The all-but-landlocked harbour of St. John's, which we saw about once a month and which afforded the barest glimpse of the sea through the Narrows, did not count. At the sight of the sea, my father always fell silent, as did the rest of us, taking our cue from him, sensing his uneasiness but having no understanding of its cause.

We went often to Ferryland to see my father's brother, Gordon, his wife, Rita, and their children. About ten miles from home the pavement ended, and the road from there was of graded gravel, the gravel plowed up on the roadside like banks of snow. Sometimes, in the summer, it was spread with a kind of faux asphalt tar to keep the dust down. It was the delusional belief of the Department of Highways that this tar slowed erosion caused by rain and retarded pothole formation. In fact the road, even in the driest summers, was cratered with potholes so large and so enduring that we gave them names. They were filled in from time to time, but it was never long before they assumed their usual dimensions; when it rained, my father eased the car suspensefully into road-wide puddles while we children, our hands and faces pressed to the back windows of the car, looked down to see how far up the water would come. When we got to Ferryland, we would examine the outside of the car for the high-water mark, which by then had dried to a mountain range of dust on the windows.

The sudden transition from pavement to gravel marked a great divide, it seemed to me, a crossing-over in both place and time, into Ferryland and into the past, my father's past. It was as if no time had gone by there since he left it. *The* past, which Ferryland was weighted down with, made it seem to me foreign or otherworldy in a way I did not then associate with time. Nor could I decide what to ascribe these sensations to, though I know now that once again it was the sea.

The primary landmarks of Ferryland were the protected part of the harbour, which from the 1600s had been called the Pool; the Downs, the expansive, seaside meadows where it was believed that Baltimore had built his mansion house; Ferryland Head, a peninsula with a manned lighthouse at its tip; Gosse Island and Bois (pronounced Boyce) Island; the two rocks that because of their shape were called the Hare's Ears, jutting a hundred feet out of the water just to the south of Ferryland Head; and the four-hundred-foot-high hill behind Ferryland whose crest was for obvious reasons known as the Gaze.

The Pool, Hare's Ears, the Downs, the Islands, Goose and Bois, Ferryland Head, the Gaze. My father recited these, invoked them as if he still oriented himself in space and time by his relation to them, the archetypal topography of Ferryland.

A further change came over my father whenever we passed through the town of Calvert and went down the hill into Ferryland, a deepening of his already sea-sombre mood. Often he fell into a brooding silence, squinting through the smoke of the cigarette that once he was under the spell of Ferryland he shunted to one side of his mouth and forgot about. He ran one hand through his hair and, puffing up his cheeks, exhaled loudly as he did in other circumstances when he doubted he could take one more minute of boredom or anxiety. It was also a signal, when he was facing some nearly unbearable prospect or situation, that he had gathered his resolve, a gesture of acknowledgment that he had no choice but to attempt something he thought he could not do. We *all* fell silent when Ferryland came into sight, especially we four boys, for we could sense what he was feeling though we could not name it and we did not know its cause. My mother gave us an explanation that we pretended to accept: my father had left Ferryland on bad terms with Charlie, because Charlie wanted him to be a fisherman and my father did not want to be one.

One day, I pointed to the house where he grew up, which was just up the road from Gordon's and where one of his sisters, Millie, and her husband now lived.

"That's the house where you were born, isn't it, Dad?" I said. It was my mother who answered.

"That's it," she said. "That was Nan's and Mr. Charlie's house." My father's parents, whom I never knew. Charlie was nine years dead when I was born. There were no pictures of him around the house, or of Nan Johnston, who died when I was three. I did not really know until I was eight or nine that everyone had two sets of grandparents.

"How come we never go there?" I said.

"It's too small inside for all of us," my mother said. "That's why Millie and Joe come visit us at Gordon's."

"But it's bigger than Gordon's," I said.

"It just looks like that from the outside," my mother said.

This transparently untrue explanation was not meant to fool me, merely to indicate that any further questions would be ignored, that this matter of "The House" was one I was not old enough to understand. "That's enough about Nan's and Charlie's now," she added, which was a warning that, even later when she was not around, we must not ask our father about it. Not that I would have. I was too awed, too fearful of the possibility that if he talked about the house, he might cry or in some way lose control.

Nan and Charlie were dead and at least partly for this reason, I presumed, were a forbidden subject. But so was my mother's mother, Lucy, dead, and we talked about her all the time.

That day my father climbed to the Gaze with his brothers, Gordon and Harold, and his sisters, Eva, Kitty and Millie, and visited the cemetery where Nan and Charlie were buried, while my mother kept us at her side in Gordon's house. Though we had gone often with our mother to Lucy's grave, we were not allowed to go with my father to see Nan's and Charlie's. With my father things were different, and there was no use asking why.

When the Johnstons came back down the hill, my father was not with them and did not return to Gordon's until half an hour later. We were told he had gone for a walk and that we were to stay put until he showed up.

Later my brothers and I went to see Nan's and Charlie's graves on our own. We climbed to the Gaze, crawled under the fence and searched among the headstones for a cluster that bore the name of Johnston and then among that cluster for "Charlie" and "May." May was Nan's real name. "Nan" was a term of endearment for grandmother, but even people not related to her called her Nan.

Their graves looked like ordinary graves to me, neither more nor less impressive than my grandmother's grave back home, except that they faced the sea. A pair of sea-facing stones, round-topped, thin, white marble stones, side by side. They were hard to read because the black had faded from their inscriptions, and all that was left were the chiselled letters which were the same white colour as the stone around them. They were older than Lucy's, too. Nan and Charlie had both died long ago; they'd crossed over into Avalon and we could there- fore never go inside the house where they had lived. Lucy, too, had crossed over into Avalon, but her house we could visit any- time we liked. It did not make sense, but that was how it was.

I looked out to sea from the Gaze. I fancied that out there, beyond what I could see, beyond the point where water and sky seemed to meet, lay the vale of Avalon to which Nan and Charlie had been borne, barge-borne by the hooded Queen and her assistant queens. Avalon was out there; it could not be as nebulously otherwordly as heaven. It had to be a material place, the ability to travel the great distance to which was made pos- sible by death. Out there, waiting, was the barge that I both dreaded and longed to see, the barge that, when Arthur died, took him to Avalon, where he was healed. The black-hooded Queen and her assistants, I assured myself, would not seem so sinister when, after I received my grievous wound, they came to get me.

Halfway up the hill behind the old house, a cartroad with a strip of wild grass growing down the centre of it led to another structure called the forge. No light had burned inside it for many years.

The forge was not off limits to us like the house. The forge my father talked about not often but fondly. And when he did, and only then, he talked about Charlie, the Charlie of his childhood. He said "Dad" as a child recounting to another the exploits of his father would have said it. He took us to the forge from which the view of Ferryland was even more spectacular than from the house.

The inside walls of the forge were stripped bare. Joe and Millie had removed and burned in their stove every piece of wood they could without bringing the roof and walls down upon themselves. The forge was a mere shell. Through the cracks in its warped clapboard the light shone, the wind shrieked. Snow gathered in shallow drifts on the floor; the rain seeped through. But Charlie's tools remained.

The all but immovable anvil was still there, its saddle gleaming as though made of silver, the rest of it burnished black and green. The anvil was encrusted with once-molten metal that had run down its sides and hardened like candle wax. Spills of reconstituted metal with borders as precise as pools of mercury lay hardened on the floor.

The anvil. The recessed stone furnace with its floor of compacted ash. The black high-fire mark still scorched on the outside of the chimney and, as far up the chute as you could see, a stretch of soot like a permanent shadow of the smoke that had poured through it day and night for years. These would remain long after the walls and anything else made of wood were gone.

My father told me the names and functions of Charlie's implements. He would walk around, pointing, explaining. Inside the forge was the forge itself, in which a bed of coals had for years burned unextinguished, smouldering but never quite going out at night. There were the bellows, the anvil, the "slack" tub or dousing tub in which finished bits were tempered in brine, the hammer and tongs. These were the obvious ones, whose functions were easy to guess. But there was also the "swage," a flat chunk of anvil-like metal with clamps, on which Charlie did his small-scale, most painstaking work, his etchings and inscriptions. There were the cutter, the chisel with its many fittings, the files and drills and the punches, which were chisel shaped but instead of attenuating to a blade had a decorative stamp on one end, a playing-card club or diamond, or Charlie's initials, CJ.

The heart punch had been Charlie's favourite. Most of his work had a little heart on it somewhere. Why he favoured the heart my father didn't know, but he showed me horseshoes bearing Charlie's trademark heart and on the other side his initials.

Once I pressed the tip of the heart punch into the palm of my hand, pressed it for so long that the shape of the heart was imprinted there. "Look what I did with the heart punch, Dad," I said, holding out my hand for him to see.

"My father died of a heart attack," my father said. It was the kind of offhand revelation he often made, telling children things that other grown-ups never would. "Nan found him. Right here in the forge." He pointed at a spot on the floor beneath the window. "Right there."

That day, on the drive back from Ferryland, I kept my hand hidden from everyone. When we got home, the print of the heart was still there. I rubbed the palm of my hand with my thumb, trying to erase the heart, but though I made my whole palm red, the heart was even redder and stood out just as clearly as before. When I went to bed, I kept my hand beneath the blankets, where I couldn't see it, but my palm tingled and I lay awake, picturing the heart, reliving the moment when I held it out for him to see. The heart punch. I was a long time getting to sleep, but I did, and when I woke up in the morning the heart was almost gone.

IN THE MORNING, when he looks out the window, the horses are lined up on the hill as always. Over breakfast, his father grumbles that the line is especially long. He will spend the first half of the day fishing, the other half making shoes and shoeing horses without a break. The day will not end for him until long after dark. He will pass the horses on his way down to the wharf where his punt is moored, and for hours while he fishes he will think of them waiting for him on the hill back home.

Men hitch their horses to the rail that runs the length of the hill, from the road past the house, then up to the forge. They go about their day's work, coming back later in the evening to claim their horses, which are now tied to the rail for finished horses on the far side of the road.

The horses and ponies stand side by side on the hill in the gloom of early morning, the zodiacal light of a sun soon to rise showing faintly in the east. The stunted Newfoundland ponies with their disproportionately large heads and overgrown blond manes move their heads from side to side, butt the larger horses out of the way so they can get their share of the hay his father spreads out on the snow. Plumes of steam issue from the noses of the animals, snorts of steam up and down the line. And steam likewise rises from the droppings they leave behind them on the path. There is so much steam it seems to be coming from the earth itself. There is a steaming trough worn in the snow by horse piss and manure, a yellow stream bed along which, before it has a chance to freeze, discoloured water flows and empties out across the road below, then farther down the hill into the Pool.

There are hundreds of horses in Ferryland, and he knows all of them by name. The wind is calm. Smoke from the chimneys and steam from the horses rise straight up in perfect columns as though the town is quiet in the aftermath of some conflagration.

He does not have to fish today. Tomorrow, but not today. On his way down to the beach, his father does not look at the horses he will have to shoe when his fishing day is done. Gordon walks behind him. After Gordon helps land the morning catch, he will go to school and be strapped for being late. His hands are so callused from hauling nets they will barely feel the blows, but to fool the nun who otherwise might find some new way of inflicting punishment he will tuck his hands in his armpits. He will grin at the other boys when she turns to face the blackboard.

Gordon tells him he should have better sense than to get up so early when he doesn't have to.

He goes up and down the line and talks to the horses, pats their necks and rubs their noses with the flat palm of his hand and feeds them kitchen scraps that he smuggled out while his mother wasn't looking, or pretended that she wasn't, for he thinks she knows he feeds the horses.

He has a special fondness for the ones who are not well cared for by their owners, the unkempt skittish ones who are little more than skin and bones and whose visits to the forge are brief respites from mistreatment or neglect. He stands with them for as much time as he can spare, for as long as he can stand the cold. He knows that when he comes home after school, the horses he is talking to will still be there, tied to the other rail, their flanks white with snow, eyelashes and nose whiskers rimed with frost.

If a horse has not been picked up by evening, his father will ask him to lead it home, for which he will receive some token of reward.

He thinks of all the horses as his father's horses. Everywhere in Ferryland he sees the prints of his father's horseshoes, in the snow, in the gravel, in the mud, in the sand on the beach below the rocks when the tide is out. Prints that bear the shapes of hearts and the initials of his father's name.

He discovered just last week that there was another blacksmith in the world, a man from a place farther south along the shore called Cappahayden whose forge they passed above on the abandoned railway line while they searched for pieces of iron for his father's rough stockpile. It looked so much like Johnston's forge he thought theirs must somehow have been moved.

As if to make up for not telling him about this second forge, his father was scornful of this other blacksmith's work.

Now he has to settle for believing that his father, though not the only blacksmith in the world, is by far the best. But what it was like to believe that his father was not *a* blacksmith but *the* blacksmith, he is unable to remember.

In the past week he noticed for the first time, though they must have been there all along, hoof prints in the snow not shaped like his father's horseshoes. He knew that horses from elsewhere had passed through, and with his boots he scuffed out the prints, erased them with the branches of spruce trees, swept the snow free of the evidence of this other black-smith, this other, rival forge and horses whose names he did not know.

After school, he looks out the window at his father in the forge, as he hammers away behind great plumes of steam on his iron anvil. The heat pours out through the open door, condenses on contact with the air.

He goes out to the forge to watch his father work. His father's right arm is much thicker than his left and out of all proportion to the rest of his body, as if it has been grafted on to him from some other man.

His father's hands move so fast his eyes can't keep up with them. The heated metal is only usable for seconds, so it has to be bent and hammered with conviction. A misshapened piece cannot be salvaged. If you are lucky, you can make something else from it, minimize your loss and make a nail from what should have been a spike.

Once the metal is removed from the furnace, his father works with the calm urgency of a surgeon bent on saving some-one's life. In the interval between the removal of the bit from the furnace and its immersion in the vat, he is oblivious to all else and something takes over that cannot be taught, something that if not for looking so simple would not work.

He hefts the bits of molten metal with a long-handled

clamp that is itself one of his creations, as are all the clamps and pliers that he uses.

His father lets him douse a bit of molten metal in the water; a sudden hiss briefly brings the water to a boil, a cloud of steam rises from the vat, obscuring the instant when the light within goes out and the transformation from ember to object occurs.

He raises a horseshoe nail still steaming from the vat, dripping water. His father takes the clamp from him and holds out the nail for him to touch. "Go on," he says, "It won't hurt."

Even though he trusts his father, he is surprised that it doesn't hurt, surprised to find that what he dipped in the vat is no longer fire but something solid, fixed and purposeful. "What happens to it in the water?" he asks.

"It gets cold."

"It doesn't just get cold," he says, convinced that his father is keeping something from him.

"It gets cold and it hardens," his father says, but he smiles as if he is harbouring some secret.

The last thing his father does is temper the nail in the briny slop of the slack tub. "Keeps it from getting rusty," he says. Then he hangs it up to dry.

His favourite contraption is the bellows, which looks like a flattened accordion with handles attached. It is made of slats of wood overlaid with leather and has all sorts of valves and pipes, levers, balances and counterbalances.

The fire has begun to burn down. He watches as his father pauses from his work to pump the bellows up to full blast. He pedals with one foot and works the handles like he is cutting grass with a massive pair of shears. Red-faced and sweating, his father concentrates on his efforts while the bellows makes its way through a series of hoots, honks and blares, climbs the musical scale until finally it begins to whistle and the fire in the forge flares up again.

From his pile of rough stock out back, his father makes runners for huge sleds used for hauling wood in the wintertime. He makes skates for his children and for all the children of Ferryland who cannot afford real skates, which is most of them. He welds and fits wagon tires, hub rings. But mostly he shoes horses.

He turns away from the fire to look at a photograph that his sister Freda took. The photograph hangs on the wall of the forge farthest from the fire. In it, their father stands outside the forge, his hands on his hips. Grimy-faced and smiling, his neck-to-foot apron making him seem even shorter and stockier than he is, he looks almost elfin, an assistant fresh from the heat and turmoil of creation, soon to cheerfully resume his task, as if all the world's implements originate from that little shack behind him. Beneath the photograph, there is a little sign that Freda made, which reads "Ferryland's Hephaestus." His father was greatly taken by it when she explained that Hephaestus was the god of the forge, the guardian of fire who made the armour of all the other gods, Zeus's thunderbolts, Achilles' shield, Diana's arrows and Europa's golden basket.

When she went away to normal school two years ago to become a teacher, Freda gave their father a book called *A History of Newfoundland* by Judge D. W. Prowse. In that book there is a letter written to Lord Baltimore by a man named Edward Wynne, the overseer of the colony at Ferryland. Dated July 28, 1622, it informs Lord Baltimore that "the Forge hath been finished this five weekes." Counting back five weeks from this date, his father concluded that the first forge in Ferryland was completed on the Feast Day of St. John the Baptist, June 24, 1622, the 125th anniversary of Cabot's landing at Cape Bonavista, and the day, in 1905, of the sighting of the Virgin Berg. His father did not read all of Prowse's history. Freda had underlined that sentence for him and put an asterisk beside it. "The Forge hath been finished this five weekes." His father considers himself to be one of a long line of blacksmiths, descended if not by blood then by trade from the unnamed smith who worked the forge in 1622.

It is Freda who talks about "the Johnston blacksmiths," as if that were their hyphenated last name, the Johnston-Blacksmiths, as if she were recounting the history of a lost line of the Johnstons that had petered out before their time. She says there have been Johnston blacksmiths in Ferryland at least since James Johnston set up shop in 1848.

In Ferryland, his father is as essential to the ceremony of matrimony as the priest. It is standard to include a blacksmith on a wedding guest list and to invite him to make a toast to the couple. It is believed he will bring good luck to the bride and groom, "forging" their union forever.

His parents have gone to every Catholic wedding in Ferryland for the past thirty years. They appear in wedding party photographs all over Ferryland. He once went into a house for the first time and was startled to see a picture of his parents on the wall above the mantelpiece.

His father didn't just learn to be a blacksmith from *his* father. He inherited, had drilled into him, a certain style of blacksmithing; he mimicked his father's choice and way of wielding tools, saw, by watching him, what the period of a hammer stroke should be, how long a certain kind of metal should be heated. He has heard people say that they can see in his father's work a kind of ghost of his grandfather's.

His father's specialty is grapnel anchors — cod-jigger-shaped, chandelier-size six-fluted anchors that are used by small-boat fishermen like himself.

He goes outside. The forge in winter is a strange meeting place of warm and cold, water and ice. Snow is falling, and a thin layer of it has collected on the roof. It gets no deeper, for it is also melting constantly. From the eaves of the forge hang icicles that, like the snow, somehow freeze and melt at once. Streams of water run from them as if from spigots.

The roof of the forge steams like a hot spring. A trench of water has built up around the base of the forge, overflowed and trickled down the hill where it has turned to a lava-like fold of ice. All winter long, a new, overlapping fold has formed with each firing of the forge, so that now the runoff is ten feet deep, a massive, discoloured, ever-growing heap of ice that his mother calls the Melt. She warns him every day to stay away from it, but he ignores her.

The shingles on the roof of the forge are glued into place with pitch, which flavours the Melt. He goes down to the Melt and breaks off a chunk of pitch-flavoured ice, goes about sucking on it like a Popsicle. His mother blames his every winter illness on the Melt. She tells him the pitch will turn his insides black as coal, asks if he has ever heard of the expression "pitch-black," tells him horses and other animals contribute to the water from which the Melt is formed, but he doesn't care. The Melt's sweet-tasting ice is free.

He goes back to the house and, hours later, looks out at the forge again. It is dark now and the little structure glows from within, the coal-fired flame of the furnace glinting blue and orange at the windows, the door closed despite the buildup of heat this causes. His father does not want the sound of his hammering to bother his neighbours, whose day is long since done.

When at last he comes in from the forge, his face is streaked with soot, rivers of black sweat run down his forearms and his neck. The undershirt he wears beneath his leather apron is drenched. His father removes his apron and, with all his strength, throws it against the wall.

"What's wrong?" Nan says.

A strange thing has happened, something his father says he has heard of but has never seen before. His anvil, at a single blow of his hammer, shattered into pieces like a block of black ice. It must have frozen to the core the night before and then thawed to the point that with one more blow of the hammer, it would crack.

He doesn't believe it. None of them do. They all run out to the forge to see if he is fooling them. He expects to find it in two or three pieces. But it seems more undone, more unmade than broken. It no longer looks like iron, let alone an anvil. It's as if a chunk of coal has been pulverized into a mound of gleaming ash.

His father says he will have to go to St. John's to get a new anvil.

"First thing tomorrow," Nan says, but his father shakes his head. The men will come as usual with their horses, and to him it is unthinkable to turn them all away. He does not say it, but they know he cannot stand the thought of the forge without an anvil, does not want it so one second longer than it has to be.

"You're not going down the Shore in the darkness by yourself," Nan says.

"Gordon can take the punt out with Uncle Will in the morning," his father says. "Art can come with me to keep me company." He tells Gordon not to let the fire in the forge go out.

"How old was that anvil?" he asks his father.

"I don't know," he says. "It used to be my father's. It's the only one I've ever had."

"Fifty years?"

"Maybe. I don't know."

They will have to travel the whole length of the Southern Shore, the forty miles of it from Ferryland to St. John's and back again, by horse and cart. His father figures they will make it back to Ferryland by noon.

It is still dark when they crest the Old Shore Road, and for the first time in his life, he sees the city of St. John's. All he can really see are lights, twin lines of lights that trace out the shapes of streets, clusters that mark neighbourhoods as large as any settlement along the Shore. The bobbing lantern lights of ships keep time with their reflections in the harbour. It makes him think of the stars as they look from his father's boat when the wind is up but the sky is clear. How could anyone bound for shore find among so many lights one to guide him safely home?

As they head down Kilbride hill, he smells the city. He is familiar with the smells of smoke and unbarked wood and salt fish, but mixed in with them are smells his father tells him come from breweries and tanneries and places where rope is made from hemp and rolled out on spools the size of wagon wheels.

When the sun comes up, so much smoke hangs in the air above St. John's that he thinks there must have been a forest fire. It hangs like a pall of morning fog between the hills that flank the harbour.

They follow the Waterford River into town. His father has not been to St. John's often enough to be able to hide how much he is intimidated by it. Their brown mare, Gail, who has made the trip just twice before, tosses her head and veers to one side each time she meets a car.

Only two cars that he knows of have ever passed through Ferryland, but here they share the street with cabriolets and buggies and men high in the saddle on shiny, sleek black horses and children riding bareback ponies.

He gapes in disbelief at the size of St. John's. His father told him it held forty thousand people, but the number is nothing next to what he sees — the cobblestone stretch of Water Street, the country's one paved road, and on it swarms of people not dressed for work as he understands the word, going in and out of what he imagines must be stores, though they look nothing like the store back home. The sheer number and size of the tall ships in the harbour strikes him dumb. He gawks at the steamers with their towering smokestacks, the barges piled high with wood and coal, the houses joined together in rows like trains without even token breaks between the cars.

Their mode of dress makes every other man look like a merchant or a minister of some kind. They wear bowler hats, long coats and vests and gleaming boots but pick their way through puddles as if their feet are bare. Women, for no reason he can think of since the sky is clear, walk about beneath umbrellas. The only umbrellas he has seen before are the ones the nuns use on rainy days, going back and forth between the convent and the church. Water Street is busier than the road below the Gaze after Sunday Mass, and it gets busier as the day goes on. How is it that with so many rushing to and from he never sees the same person twice?

He waits for his father outside the gates of the foundries, stares at the streams of men who come and go, waits for his father to appear, holding Gail by the bridle because he knows that as soon as she sees him she will kick up her forelegs and might break her harness. It is in part his nervousness that makes her restless. Every so often he feeds her the stalk of a carrot or turnip. To thank him she butts him with her head.

They go from foundry to foundry in search of an anvil.

He doesn't know what his father is looking for in an anvil, though his father assures him that no two anvils are alike. He watches from a distance as his father, who has brought a hammer, strikes several dozen anvils experimentally, almost diagnostically, searching for one that will make the hammer rebound to his satisfaction and return the force of the blow into his body in a way that feels indefinably right.

Each time he tests an anvil, a man stands beside him, watching. Once, when his father is done, he and the man confer, the man looking at his father, his father at the anvil until at last he shakes his head and walks away.

"What was wrong with that one?" he asks.

"I'll come back for it unless I find a better one," his father says.

Finally his father emerges from a foundry to announce that he has chosen his anvil. Three men wheel it on a trolley to the gate while his father walks beside it.

He thought he would get to see up close what a new anvil looked like, but this one is far from new. It looks much older than his father's. The saddle has begun to rust. It must be years since it was last struck with a hammer. His father scours out the swage fitting and the clamp holes with a file until water poured in one end comes out the other.

"There. There's nothing wrong with that," his father says. "I'll burn off that rust when we get home."

After several men help him load it onto the cart, they set out for Ferryland, the canvas-covered anvil like a catafalque, Gail plodding with what looks like funereal restraint, though they know she is going as fast as she can. He is hungry and wonders if he should ask his father if they can stop somewhere to get a loaf of bread. For the first time he wonders how much the anvil set them back.

The short winter day is over, and it is getting dark again when they leave the city limits and reach the Old Shore Road. The number of cars and trucks and carriages and buggies on the gravel road grows fewer the farther up the Shore they go. At a certain point, once they have passed through Kilbride, the Goulds, the road to Petty Harbour, his father drops the reins and lets Gail go at her own pace; she knows the way and needs no guidance unless the roads are bad.

They sit in silence for a while as she clops along. Then his father gives what for him is a speech of record length. "There'll be no more need for blacksmiths soon," his father says. "There's not as many horses as there used to be. Soon there'll be almost none at all. What shoes they need they'll make in foundries by the hundreds. They'll make anchors there, grapnels like I make, but they'll make them a lot faster than I do. Everything I make they'll make it there but ten times faster."

He tells him that he was apprenticed to *his* father when he was twelve, "your age," he says. But there will be, in the Johnston family, no more such apprenticeships, for blacksmithing is a trade that in cities is already obsolete and halfway to becoming so in Ferryland, where horses are being replaced by cars and trucks and where many people are buying their metal implements from foundries that mass-produce them in St. John's. Blacksmithing is a craft that over several thousand years hardly changed, and over the past fifty has been abandoned.

He looks around. He thinks his father must be wrong. Even here in the city horses still outnumber cars and trucks. He cannot imagine Ferryland ever having more need for cars than horses, or the men of Ferryland ever preferring shoes made in foundries to shoes made in the forge.

"You'll have to find yourself something else to do," his father says. "You'll be better off at something else."

"What will I do?" he says.

"You could be a fisherman," his father says. "There's not many that can make a go of it without something on the side, but you might be able to."

He has been going out in the punt every other morning for two years now with his father and his older brother, Gordon. It will be two more years before he has to go out every morning. They work the nets and traps and leave the handlining to him. It is no easier but less dangerous than what they do. He baits the hooks with squid and capelin, plays out the handline to twenty or thirty fathoms, but he is not yet strong enough to haul in even that much line without their help, especially on a good day, when the hooks are full. When he looks down into the water, he can see the hooked fish at fathom intervals, their white cod bellies bent almost in half, first one way, then the other as they fight for freedom. He is still astonished each time the first cod, in a flapping fury, breaks the surface.

His father and Gordon laughed so hard they had to stop working once when he wrestled into the boat a codfish half his size. It was so wide and plump he could barely clutch it to his chest. He put his arms around it from behind, clasped his hands across its slimy belly, but it kept sliding back into the water. Time after time he hefted it up, all the while trying to keep out of the way of its thrashing head and sharp fins that beat like wings. It seemed since he had pulled it from the water to have sprouted fins all over. They drenched him in a fine mist of salt spray that stung his eyes. Its mouth, because his arms were entangled in its gills, was wide open. He could see inside but all he noticed was its teeth. He thought for a few seconds that he had hooked the wrong kind of fish, not a cod but some deep-sea sculpin his father should have warned him he might catch by accident. He knew that if he let go of the fish the line they had already pulled in would play out so fast there would be no time to avoid the hooks as they went flying from the boat. At last he heaved the cod's lower half from the water and fell on his back into the boat, the codfish likewise on top of him. The fish was so cold he could barely stand the touch of it against his skin. How could anything so lively be so cold? He was amazed that something so large made no sound, its silence at odds with the fury of its struggle. "He's in the boat. You can let go of him now," his father said. He rolled out from under the fish, which lay there, more subdued now, gills working uselessly, dark eyes unmoving as if up here it could not see. He looked at the water. From the unimaginable bottom of the ocean it had come and now lay stranded in the boat because of him.

Afterwards his forearms were rubbed raw and flecked with silver scales and his face was nicked all over with tiny cuts.

He has never once gone on the water without getting sick, but he never gets sick more than once a trip, no matter how rough it gets. These are the terms of the peculiar bargain he has already made with the sea. It is necessary for him to be sick once and only once on each trip before he gets his sea legs. His father and his brother are so used to it they pay not the slightest attention to him as their boat puts out to sea in the early morning darkness and he heaves over the side as though performing some routine act of hygiene.

Freda tells him in her letters it is not so much his body as his mind that performs this daily ritual, this demonstration of revulsion for the water that, though it might have him for the moment, will not always have him. She does not think he should be a fisherman. She thinks he should find something that will make it unnecessary for him to ever again go on the water. Though he has not told anyone else, he agrees with her, but he has not yet decided what that something is. "The whole world is not like Newfoundland," she wrote. "There are other places you can go. Not everybody stays."

His father stops talking. They move along the old road and despite the wartime blackout light the buckboard lanterns.

They see, by their lights or by the clouds of dust they raise, other carts, carriages and vehicles from miles away, and hail every one they meet. They smell the sea on one side and the spruce trees on the other, gauge their progress by the towns they pass through. His father counts them off, announcing each one like a train conductor. Kilbride, the Goulds, Big Pond, Bay Bulls, Witless Bay, Mobile, Burnt Cove, Lamanche, Bauline, Cape Broyle, Calvert — the litany of place names that will bring them back from the city to the place where they were born.

They climb the hill and cross the flats of Old Bay Bulls until the road again descends to the beach at Witless Bay. All along the Southern Shore, the beaches lie at the mouths of ancient rivers that have worn fissures and valleys and fjord-like indentations in the headlands, and natural breakwaters of beach rocks have been piled up by ten thousand years of waves, piled so high that at sea level he cannot see the water, only a crescent of rocks beyond which he can dimly hear the ocean.

They cross the dark, empty stretches between one town and the next, the moonlit stretch of barrens strewn with ice-caught ponds above Bay Bulls, the phosphorescent glow along the bays where no one lives, bays with names his father doesn't bother to announce, the tree-crowded mile of road before the turnoff to Lamanche, where Gail becomes skittish, picking up the scent of a lynx or a weasel in the woods.

By the time they reach Calvert, it has begun to snow. Both he and his father fall asleep and do not wake up even when Gail turns into the merchant's driveway and begins to ascend the hill below the store. The shopkeeper looks out the window and sees

Gail standing in the light of the porch lantern, for how long he has no idea, waiting for someone to notice. A man and a boy are sound asleep against the buckboard, heads slumped forward onto their chests, snow gathering on their hats and shoulders and on their folded arms.

He wakes up first and nudges his father awake. "We're at O'Brien's," he says.

His father looks around, then nods. "Gail's tired too," he says. "She took the first turnoff that she recognized. Just as well. We need some things."

Wiping the snow from their clothes, they leave Gail untethered and go inside the store, where the fire in the stove in the middle of the floor is barely lit. The sun is not yet up. They are the first customers.

The fish merchant's store. He loves coming here. He walks among the shelves, looks at the squares of fresh fudge laid out uncovered on waxed paper, the sugar-sprinkled wedges of mint green and orange ju-jubes, jawbreakers that a boy at school told him change colour by the minute in your mouth, jagged chunks of chocolate in glass jars, bins of jelly beans, striped bars of peppermint and long black twists of licorice, the stacks of oranges and "five-point" apples. He feels his hunger so keenly that he has to grab on to a shelf to keep from falling.

"Help you with something over there?" the man behind the counter says. Embarrassed, he shakes his head, looks for something the man will not mind him standing next to.

"You don't have to watch him," his father calls from the back room, where the bulk goods and the fishing gear are stored. He knows they will leave the great emporium with nothing but bulk bags of staples like oats and flour.

"Oh no. No, of course not," the man says and looks out the window as if he has just now noticed what an interesting horse and cart they have.

His father comes out from the back room with a sack of oats and a bag of flour. He joins him at the counter. He dreads what he knows is coming next.

The clerk opens his credit book and deducts the purchases and reads aloud to his father how much credit they have left. In this store, money never changes hands. For the fish he catches and sells to the merchant, his father is given credit here. This, he knows, is called the "truck" system. He knows that the merchant devalues the credit at will by raising the prices of the goods he sells. He also knows that the man behind the counter is not the merchant, just someone who works for him. They see the man who owns the store once a week at Sunday Mass.

"We should have more credit left than that," his father says. At first it seems this is just a token protest. He wonders again how much the anvil set them back and where his father found the money for it. The most money he has ever seen in his father's hands is a ten-cent piece.

The man behind the counter shakes his head.

"That's what it says here, Mr. Johnston," the clerk says, pointing at the bottom line below his father's name. His father nods, pauses as if to speak, exhales heavily, puts both hands on the edge of the counter and looks down as if considering some course of action. Then, abruptly, he sweeps the ledger off the counter with both hands. It lands somewhere out of sight. He hears it slide along the floor until, with a thump, it hits the wall.

The clerk steps back from the counter. "There's no need for that," he says.

"Dad," he says and puts his hand on his father's arm and looks up into his face.

His father turns sharply away, stoops down and picks up the oats and the flour, carries them out to the cart and jams them in beside the anvil. He climbs up and sits slump-shouldered on the buckboard. The rope reins lie between his feet. Gail shakes her harness bells. His eyes shut as if, upon resuming his former pose, he has gone back to sleep. He grips the upper part of his huge right arm with his left hand, squeezes it as if the muscle has begun to ache.

He's still not sure it's over. He's not sure until, when he climbs up beside him, his father opens his eyes, looks at him and says, "I wonder will we ever get the country back. When the war is over maybe."

"Once we had a country, but because we made a mess of it, the British took it back." Freda's words. She said that from 1855 to 1934, Newfoundland was a self-governing colony of Britain. "Just a fancy phrase for country," his father said. Since 1934 when it had, because of helping Britain win the war, not a penny to its name, the British were "in charge." "In charge" is how he thinks of it. He is not sure what it means.

"Things might not be any better if we get it back," his father says. "They might be worse."

"They'll be better," he says.

"Will they? You got it all figured out?"

He nods solemnly.

His father laughs.

He remembers the sound the ledger made as it slid along the floor. He knows that the next time they go the man behind the counter will pretend it never happened.

"Nan will fry us up some toutons," his father tells him as Gail returns to the road. Toutons. Pan-fried balls of bread that, as Nan says, fill you up like Christmas dinner. He can't wait to get back home.

"You're not going to school," his father says. "I'll tell the teacher that you're sick."

"Can I stay out in the forge?" he says.

"Sure," his father says. "You can lead the horses back and forth."

Not for another ten years will he see for the second time the city that prompted his father to predict a day when there would be more cars than horses in the streets.

He will think of it often but they will never speak of it again.

I WAS BORN in St. John's, but my parents moved to my mother's hometown, the Goulds, when I was one.

My mother's people, the Everards, were from Petty Harbour, which is now the postcard outport of Newfoundland, primarily because of its close proximity to St. John's. You can drive to Petty Harbour from St. John's in fifteen minutes by way of a coastal road that wasn't there when my mother was growing up.

The Everards took pride in the fact that from nowhere in the Goulds could you see the town of Petty Harbour or the ocean.

My mother's people were not of the water, very much not of the water, though their most recent ancestors were. They were very much of the land, such as it was, sea-scorners, sea-fearers, one rung up the social ladder of the lower classes by dint of their non-association with the sea, with merchants and the truck system and because what they harvested they had themselves created and so they did not have to depend for their livelihood on the whims of such a lowly, bottom-feeding creature as the cod.

The Everards had moved inland from Petty Harbour in the late nineteenth century, when the fishing grounds became too crowded. The first of them to move still fished part-time, maintaining summer shacks in Petty Harbour or nearby Shoal Bay, at the same time farming in the Goulds.

My grandfather and some other settlers cleared the wilderness of trees and rocks. My grandfather must have been either a late migrant or an indiscriminate one, for although there was much flatland in the Goulds, he situated his farm on the side of a hill. The angle of the furrows to the vertical was more than forty-five degrees on the steepest meadow, which had to be plowed from the bottom up because a horse going downhill could not keep its feet.

The labour that went into clearing this land I could not, did not, begin to imagine. It never occurred to me as a child that the farm had not always been there, never occurred to me to wonder why there was a meandering wall of stones along each cartroad, or how what we called "the stump meadow," a bog in which hundreds of uprooted stumps lay slowly rotting or ossified by age, had come to be.

The Goulds was much younger than Ferryland. It had no historic sites or plaques, no stone churches from another century, had not grown from a colony founded by some aristocrat from England, had no founding heroes at all that were commemorated in books, no town museum. The Goulds, in New World terms, was anomalously new and anomalously agricultural.

But although it was not as old as Ferryland, the Goulds felt and looked older, because the remnants of its first generation lay not, as they are in Ferryland, so deeply buried that the place is now a favourite digging site for archaeologists, but above ground, in plain view — the empty shells of long-abandoned barns and cellars that you could see straight through still stood at angles to the ground, as did fences built for some forgotten purpose, their posts supported by the grey-washed stones that, within someone's living memory, had been uprooted from the ground. There were already by my time farms that looked the way my grandfather's does now, failed, long-abandoned farms, open fields where hay and fodder that no one bothered with grew wild, fallen fence posts still joined by wire, stands of stunted, wind-bent junipers along the road, grown up since the levelling of spruce and birch. In one place, criss-crossed by paths where we played and took shortcuts to school, a mature forest had arisen on land that must have been among the first to be cleared a hundred years ago. The rocks pried from the earth were piled in heaps that now were all but overgrown by moss.

We wandered my grandfather's farm on Sunday afternoons when he was sleeping, played among trucks left for good where they had broken down and been deemed beyond repair, among discarded farm implements, ploughshares without handles, handles without blades, tires complete with rims from some early version of the tractor. There were old hubcaps nailed to trees. Rain-greyed lengths of rope that had been used to tether livestock hung from branches. Upside-down paint cans had been stuck on fence posts for target practice. On the ground lay rusting coils of chains. We were on orders from my grandfather not to move any of these things, as if they had been placed with a purpose. His history in the Goulds was commemorated haphazardly throughout the farm by unculled artifacts.

The only constant in the Goulds was the contour of the land: the land as it looked in winter, shorn of most of its vegetation, shorn down to bedrock; the hills beyond the farms that bound the town on every side but west, where lay one leg of the bog of Avalon. The hills were so far above the town they were merely dark green shapes, at night bald silhouettes against the sky.

My grandfather's farm seemed to me a vast place. To go to the uppermost hayfield, beyond the pound, beyond the grazing field, beyond the crops, beyond the fodder, was a great, rarely embarked upon adventure. But the last time I was there, a few years ago, it took me less than ten minutes to climb to the top of the hill. As I looked down at the site of the old house and barn, it seemed impossible that a man and a woman had supported themselves and their seven children on the annual yield of that barely arable few acres and the milk produced by a dozen cows.

It was into this farming family that my father married, in this farming town he eventually settled, among farmers-in-law who held forever in reserve the trump card of irony that a man of his particular field of specialization — he was an agricultural technologist — ended up working for the fisheries while they were growing crops and raising cows without the benefit of a diploma in anything.

BY 1963, IT was estimated that expatriate Newfoundlanders and their descendants numbered two million, or four times the population of the province. "A country's worth" of Newfoundlanders lived abroad, my father said.

During the war, thousands of Newfoundland women married and went back to the States with American servicemen. All but one of my mother's five aunts scattered to the Boston States.

My grandfather received news of his sister May's death after not having seen or heard from her for fifty years, though there had been no falling-out between them. He was sixty years old at the time. It was summer. My mother and I went to see him after my grandmother called, but I was six, so my mother told me nothing. My grandmother was in the kitchen when we got there. I wandered off down the hallway. The door of my grandparents' bedroom was open, and my grandfather was sitting on his bed, hands resting on the edge of the mattress, shoulders slumped. I was shocked to see him indoors on a weekday afternoon. Sunshine poured into the room, illuminating dust motes and a patch of ancient rug.

"Hello, Wayne," he said.

"How come you're in here?" I said.

"Just thinking about May," he replied. I thought he meant the month of May. I was about to ask for an explanation when my mother found me and brought me back to the kitchen.

It was an unprecedented lapse for any grown-up that I knew, but especially for one as notoriously "hard" as he was, to admit what he had to a child. He had been ten when May left home. She had been a girl of seventeen, which must have been how he remembered her. He had got the news less than an hour before, had been called in from the fields by my grandmother when she came back from the post office with a letter addressed to him from Boston. She must have known its contents. It was just a question of which of his sisters had died.

Half an hour after I saw him sitting on the bed, he came out through the kitchen, went to the fridge, filled a bottle with ice-cold water from a jug, stoppered the bottle and went back to work.

None of my great-aunts ever came back home. It was as if they had gone to a place from which Newfoundland seemed so other-worldly they had stopped believing it was real. Home, when they left it, had ceased to exist.

For my part, I did not believe in *them*, these great-aunts whom I had never seen and who had supposedly lived longer in the Goulds than I had lived so far. It seemed to me they must have been only shadowy presences who had faded so slowly away that their final departure had been barely noticed.

Realizing that Newfoundland's greatest tourism potential lay in enticing expatriates back home to the island, Premier Joey Smallwood designated 1966 as Come Home Year. It was a kind of amnesty, as if, on behalf of their relatives who could not bring themselves to do it, the government had declared to prodigal sons and daughters who had gone to the mainland to find work that all was forgiven, there were no hard feelings.

A campaign to induce homesickness in expatriates was launched. The time was right for it. A new kind of music that had been invented by homesick Newfoundlanders was forever playing on the radio. My father called it "the green-arsed baymen blues." It spoke, he said, to the homesick, city-sick, pal-pining, mother-missing, sweetheart-yearning, mainland-stranded baymen.

Come Home Year licence plates were issued. Ads were run in newspapers in Toronto, Boston, New York and even London, England, where a lot of Newfoundlanders lived who had not been home since the end of the Second World War.

It was because the first paved cross-province highway was completed in 1966 that that year was designated Come Home Year. It was the showcase accomplishment of provincial-federal co-operation, for one thing, and for another allowed people who could not afford to fly their families home to make the trip by car and ferry.

In the summer of 1966, Newfoundlanders from all over the world came home for the province-wide reunion. It seemed there was at least one long-lost this or that in everybody's house, the place crawling with nostalgia-ridden, reminiscence-mad expatriates with mainland accents introducing their main-land-born children to their grandparents for the first time.

Everywhere people were making up with one another and pledging never to have a falling-out again and that from now on they would keep in touch. There was a kind of surprise reunion craze that summer, and along with it a kind of reunion paranoia, everyone, even those who were themselves planning something, suspecting that something was being planned for them. The slightest deviation from the norm aroused suspicion. It got so that anyone who had relatives who had moved to the mainland was afraid to open a door for fear of finding them behind it. I remember a boy in our neighbourhood telling us there was an epidemic of heart attacks brought on by reunions, that Newfoundlanders all over were dropping dead from sheer surprise.

These Newfoundlanders had been told by relatives or had read in ads placed in mainland newspapers that they were coming home to a new Newfoundland, the post-Confederation Newfoundland so different from the one they had left that they would hardly recognize it. They were told that once they saw that Newfoundland no longer lagged behind the rest of the world, they would want to stay for good.

Some Newfoundlanders did come back for good during the summer of Come Home Year, among them my uncle Dennis, my mother's brother, who had left for Toronto just after we joined Confederation in 1949 and had not been home since.

There was a welcome home party for Dennis at my uncle Harold's. (Harold was my father's younger brother; his wife, Marg, was my mother's sister.) He met a horde of nieces and nephews he had never seen before and introduced to us his Ontario-born wife and daughter. Dennis, after seventeen years of working on a loading dock in Toronto, came back to join his father and his brother Gerald on the family farm. He was forever describing to us children the wonders of Toronto but ignored us when we brazenly asked him why, if Toronto was so wonderful, he had come back home.

All the Johnstons and the Everards and their spouses and children were at the Come Home Year Party. My father's sister, Eva, and her husband, Jim, were there. They were famous among the family for walking out whenever "O Canada" was played. Eva lived in St. John's, so I myself had never witnessed one of these walkouts, but each time she and Jim staged one I heard about it.

The grown-ups gathered in the front room while we children were relegated to the kitchen. I stood in the doorway between the two rooms and watched them, sensing a momentousness that had to do with more than just Come Home Year. This was the largest gathering of my relatives that I had ever seen. I was eight and knew from past experience that when more than four or five of them gathered in one place, it was inevitable that they would get going about Confederation.

Almost anything could get my father going about it at almost any time. He would start off complaining about having the flu or about how awful the weather was and somehow wind up on the subject, though it was eighteen years since our side had been defeated in the referendum, since Newfoundlanders had renounced independence by a heartbreakingly small margin.

He held forth at the party in ruefully aggrieved, reverential tones about Peter Cashin, whom he said was one of the greatest public speakers who ever lived, a man who, when it came to making speeches, "put Joey Smallwood to shame." There hung on our wall, facing you in the porch as you entered, a black-and-white portrait of Cashin, the closest thing to a leader the factious anti-confederates had had.

My grandfather Charlie had been a friend and supporter of Major Cashin's, one of many lieutenants who worked with him in the referendum. Charlie had witnessed the confrontation that had brought the young Cashin local fame, a fight with a nun named Sister Joseph, who was so large she could not pass through doors except sideways. No one who had not seen them square off at the start would have known whom she was fighting with, so quickly did they wind up on the ground and so rarely and fleetingly did Cashin appear from among the manifold layers of her habit. It looked as if she had thrown a fit and with all the strength that God could spare her for the purpose was trying to subdue some devil with whom she was invisibly possessed. You could have made, from what she wore, a hundred pairs of pants for the Major, Charlie said, as if by that to estimate how badly he was overmatched. It ended suddenly, audibly, with a thud and Sister Joseph splayed supine, on her face a look of stern bewilderment, Cashin somewhere beneath her. When she got up, the young Cashin did not. Her breastplate of celluloid was in two places broken and her wooden cross hung down her back. Her nose was bleeding, her chin and cheekbones bruised, while Cashin, nun-pummelled, unconscious, was unmarked.

My father described how, just before making a speech, Cashin would roll up his shirtsleeves and smash his fist on the table or desk in front of him. This was easy to believe from his portrait, which appeared to have been taken by a photographer the breaking of whose neck Cashin had postponed just long enough to let him take his picture. The stocky, fierce-looking Major, a hero of the First World War, stared from the photograph as if daring you to say the word "Confederation."

Harold's wife, Marg, described how in her haste to get home and hear Cashin speaking on the radio, she'd tripped and broken her leg. That was the kind of loyalty, the kind of fervour the Major inspired.

My father quoted, in denunciation of Smallwood, the observation made by Parnell in his famous speech at Cork, Ireland, in 1885: "No man has the right to fix the boundary of the march of a nation; no man has a right to say to his country, thus far shalt thou go and no further."

They all saw Cashin as a Parnell-like figure, after whose defeat by some conspiracy that, though "common knowledge," was impossible to prove, everything went bad.

"Who was Parnell?" I asked.

"A great leader for Irish independence," my father said. "Hounded to his death by priests because he had a fling with a married woman named Kitty O'Shea."

"What's a fling?"

"A sinfully delicious piece of pastry," Uncle Harold said.

"We ruled ourselves for eighty years," my father said. "From 1855 to 1934. And then that bloody British Commission of Government was set up. To save us, they said. To save Newfoundland from going bankrupt."

And then he got on to Joey Smallwood, who was leader of the confederates at the National Convention from 1946 to 1948. The National Convention was an assembly elected to decide what forms of government should be offered to the people of

Newfoundland in a referendum. The Convention voted not to include Confederation with Canada on the ballot, but Whitehall ruled that it should be included anyway.

"Everybody knows the referendum was rigged," my father said. England, supposed to be neutral on the issue, had been in cahoots with Canada, and Canada had been in cahoots with Joey; all of them, in some way that my father deemed to be past my understanding, had rigged the referendum.

I watched my father and noted how the grown-ups watched him, hanging on his every word as Cashin's followers must have hung on his in the 1940s. He seemed to me no less a leader than his namesake, King Arthur, or Parnell or Cashin, all the more impressive for being, as each of them had been, the patron of a lost, just cause.

"Even with it rigged, they barely won," he said scornfully, as if the nearness of the vote somehow proved that it was rigged. "I can tell you this much — if Newfoundland had stayed a country and Peter Cashin had become prime minister —"

"He would have done away with fog and drizzle," Uncle Dennis said. I thought this was pretty funny, but the silence that followed this remark was so censorious Dennis didn't speak another word for hours. He had gone away to Canada — as the Canadian mainland was still referred to by members of my family, though we had been Canadians for twenty years — and it had taken him seventeen years to see the error of his ways. Not many remarks of this kind would have been tolerated from anyone, but especially not from him.

As I regarded them, it seemed possible, even inevitable, that Confederation would somehow be undone. How could anything stand when so many grown-ups were against it? They were still able to summon up some scorn, some indignation, still able to suspend their disbelief in the reversibility of Confederation and act as if they would no longer put up with having had their country taken from them.

"One thing is certain," my father said, "and that is this: all who voted for Newfoundland did so out of love for Newfoundland. Are we agreed on that point?" They all gave their vigorous assent, nodding their heads, Uncle Dennis, trying to make amends for his gaffe of a moment ago, Uncle Harold and Uncle Jim flanking my father, their eyes averted from his as if to indicate how intently they were listening. They wound up in a close circle around him, holding their glasses, smoking, Harold and Jim rising up ever so slightly on their toes from time to time in a way that was somehow linked to the rhythm of my father's voice, as though they were urging him on, as though he was rolling now. Whenever my father made some point, Aunt Marg looked at my mother as if to say, There now, there it is — at last someone has said it. My father began speaking as though someone present was opposing him, though no one was.

"Now," my father said, "of those who voted for Confederation, of how many can it be said that they did so out of love for Canada?" At this, Uncle Harold and Uncle Jim pursed their lips doubtfully.

"The numbers tell the tale," my father said.

"Indeed they do," said Aunt Marg.

"Confederation seventy-eight thousand," my father said, "Responsible Government seventy-one thousand. A mere seven-thousand-vote difference. Now, if only thirty-five hundred, and it was surely ten times that, but if only thirty-five hundred who voted for Confederation did so, not because they ceased believing in Newfoundland, but, shall we say, for economic reasons. That is to say, if they voted —" he paused for effect — "reluctantly" — Uncle Harold and Uncle Jim nodded — "regretfully" — they nodded again — "half-heartedly, even self-ashamedly —" He all but spat out this last word. My uncles nodded more emphatically than ever.

"Do you see what I'm getting at?" my father said. "If the answer is as few as thirty-five hundred, and it is surely ten times that, we are left with the conclusion that in their heart of hearts, a vast majority of Newfoundlanders still believe in Newfoundland."

There was an emphatic murmur of assent.

"How many Newfoundlanders, if they thought they had nothing to gain financially from joining Canada, would have voted to join? What would they be voting for? Who knew anything about Canada in 1949? It was patriotism versus pragmatism. And God help us, ladies and gentlemen, pragmatism won."

"Patriotism versus pragmatism," said Uncle Harold, nodding, then shaking his head as if to say, You have put into words as I myself could not have done the very essence of my thinking on the matter.

"Patriotism versus pragmatism," said Uncle Jim, as if it was hard to believe that because of those two words we lost it all.

My father moved on to what he called the closet confederates. There were many people, he was convinced, who had outwardly opposed Confederation and, indeed, opposed it in their heart of hearts but in the secrecy of the ballot box had voted for it.

"Imagine," my father said, "having to go your entire life living with a lie. Pretending to your wife or your father or your sister or your best friend that you were on their side, that you had voted with them, and knowing, knowing in your heart of hearts that in that voting booth, when no one else was looking, you betrayed them."

"Oh yes, my God yes, the closet confederates," Uncle Harold said, as if he had forgotten about them, as if, now that he had been reminded of them, a flood of memory had been released and it was as if he was back there, in the wake of defeat, in a world full of closet confederates and broken-hearted patriots. He shook his head, eyes downcast, as if no worse fate could be imagined than to be a member of that phantom faction. Everyone denounced the closet confederates in some manner. You had to, I suppose, and fervently, or else be suspected of being one. It was somehow comforting, reassuring to them, the impossible-to-verify idea that there existed this group of tortured, self-betraying souls.

"Don't go on about them now, Arthur," Aunt Eva said. "I can't even stand to think about them, the poor things, the hell, the living hell their lives must be."

"You're right, my dear," my father said. "The less said about that crowd the better."

"They made their beds, now let them lie," said Uncle Dennis. No one endorsed this remark. He looked as if he was beginning to realize what he had let himself in for by coming back to Newfoundland.

"And the Terms of Union that Smallwood negotiated with Canada..." my father continued. He explained that under these terms, Newfoundland was forbidden to market

wa y n e   j o h n s t o n

its yellow margarine in Canada, where the sale of it was against
the law.

"What does that tell us about Canadians, Art?" Uncle
Harold said, as he often did whenever Canada was mentioned.

My father gave the answer he always gave: "If inquired
into, Harold, it might tell us much about Canadians, but one's
time would more usefully be spent cataloguing in Latin every
species of fly that has ever pitched on or sought entrance to the
arsehole of a cow."

They laughed, then fell silent for a while.

"I'll tell you one thing I would love to know," my father
said. "And that is, what was in Brown's Document?"

"Wouldn't we all?" Aunt Eva said, as if a fierce desire to
know the contents of Brown's document was universal. I had
never heard of Brown's Document before.

"Oh yes, my God yes, Brown's Document," Uncle Harold
said. "Yes, I remember that now, Brown's Document. What
was that all about now, Art?"

Brown was Kenneth Brown, an ardent anti-confederate
and elected member of the National Convention, the delegate
for Bonavista South. Delegates to the National Convention
sat in alphabetical order according to the names of their
constituencies, so Brown sat next to Gordon Bradley, member
for Bonavista East, the Convention chairman and a confederate, and next to Bradley sat Joe Smallwood, member for
Bonavista Centre.

At a crucial point in the Convention, Brown rose and,
while making a passionate speech opposing Smallwood's motion
to send a delegation to Ottawa to find out what Canada would
offer a confederated Newfoundland, took from his pocket a

– 6 0 –

"document" and, waving it about, declared that if he were to reveal its contents, not a single delegate or Newfoundlander would vote for Confederation. Just on the verge of revealing the contents of the document, Brown collapsed, all six feet four of him, onto the floor in front of his desk. He had a massive stroke. In the confusion that followed, as delegates rushed to his aid and ambulance attendants arrived, Brown's Document somehow disappeared.

"No trace of it was ever found," my father said, adding that Brown never did recover from his stroke to the point that he could think or speak clearly enough to make anyone understand what was in the document.

My father seemed to think the disappearance of the document was no mystery, given that Smallwood and Bradley were sitting closest to Brown when he collapsed. But what *was* the document? What information did it contain? What could have had the effect that Brown predicted, could have caused all Newfoundlanders, even declared confederates like Smallwood, to turn their backs on Confederation? They speculated endlessly about it. The Home Office. Canadian Prime Minister Mackenzie King. Britain's man in Newfoundland, Governor MacDonald. The "Commissioners Three," as my father called the three British members of the Commission of Government appointed to rule Newfoundland after the country's brush with bankruptcy in 1934. Joe Smallwood. All these names came up in their speculations. The document might have been part of some conspiracy-revealing correspondence between some or all of these.

And there was the stroke itself, so eerily timed to cut Brown short just when he was on the brink of revelation. One

could hardly blame the confederates for his stroke, but still...
My father shook his head and everyone lapsed into silence as if
in wonderment at what might have been had Brown not had his
stroke and Brown's Document not disappeared. I could just see
the great figure of Brown falling with a kind of tragic grace,
splendidly laid out on the floor still clutching the document that
might have saved us, the document whose contents he alone was
privy to and that somehow in the next few seconds disappeared.

There were many possible explanations, of course, which
they begrudgingly proposed and then discounted. Brown had
merely been exaggerating for effect — the document was probably inconsequential. But Brown was not known for stooping to
such tactics. And he was no fool. He would have known better
than to discredit himself in such a manner. Was it possible,
then, that just seconds from a massive stroke, Brown was expe-
riencing some sort of pre-stroke delusion, his brain already suf-
fering its effects? But he had been, however animated, quite
lucid while making his speech, and had correctly followed par-
liamentary procedure when he rose to speak against
Smallwood's motion.

Perhaps in the certainty of being assured that she was
wrong, Aunt Eva wondered if the whole thing might have have
been an act of divine intervention, if God had stepped in to save
the confederates just when their cause was about to be
destroyed. It was the consensus that while it was impossible to
say what God's purpose was in striking down poor Brown, it
had most certainly not been to advance the cause of Joey
Smallwood. Then, in a contradiction of this assertion that went
unnoticed or ignored, it was observed that Brown's stroke, the
loss of the referendum, Confederation were the acts of a God

Baltimore's Mansion

whose ways were inscrutable to man, apparent injustices that in fact were part of some divine plan so grand in its benignity and scope that for mere men to inquire into it was pointless. Why could God not have given Brown a few more minutes? We would no more know the answer to that question than we would know what was in the document.

The fact was that Brown's Document had divine intervention written all over it, if one believed in such a thing. They did, or were at least capable of suspending their disbelief in it from time to time. And so Brown's Document was a problem. It stood on the one hand for the nagging, never-to-be-spoken-aloud notion that their side was in the wrong, that Brown's stroke was a sign of God's disfavour with the cause of independence. On the other hand, it perfectly embodied their abiding sense of grievance, of having been hard done by, cheated for all time out of what was rightfully theirs by unseen human hands.

"Brown's Document" was a phrase that invoked for me the world view of Malory's *Morte d'Arthur*, that the true king was always in exile while some pretender held the throne, that the honourable, by virtue of their being honourable, must always lose. Brown lay on the floor, his long journey to the vale of Avilion begun, having suffered, like King Arthur, a grievous head wound from which he could not recover.

It was not Malory my father was thinking of, but another poet. My father, as in the years to come he would often do when the two of us talked about such things, quoted Yeats's poem "To a Friend Whose Work Has Come to Nothing," which Lady Gregory told Yeats was her favourite poem and that she pitied the poor "friend" mentioned in the title. After Lady Gregory's death, Yeats revealed she was this friend. My father recited it as a tribute to the Major: "For how can you compete,/Being honour bred, with one/Who, were it proved he lies,/Were neither shamed in his own/Nor in his neighbour's eyes?"

As the party wore on, they moved from one referendum story to another. They got a lot of mileage out of Newfoundland's having become a part of Canada on April Fools' Day and would not suffer anyone to argue that induction day was in fact March 31. The induction ceremonies were originally set for April Fools' Day 1949, it having occurred to no one at the federal level that this might not be the most appropriate of dates until Joey Smallwood brought it to their attention. The date was then, at the eleventh hour, "changed." In fact, it was too late to really change it, since all sorts of ceremonies had already been set for April 1 on Parliament Hill, but Canadian Prime Minister Louis St. Laurent amended the Terms of Union by which Newfoundland joined Canada to read that Newfoundland would join the Dominion not immediately after midnight but "immediately before the expiration of March 31, 1949." Thus were Newfoundlanders robbed of an infinitesimal fraction of a second of independence and by that same infinitesimal fraction of a second supposedly spared the humiliation of having to commemorate their joining the Dominion on April Fools' Day. All the ceremonies in Newfoundland and Ottawa took place on April 1, however, and many people, especially those descended from anti-confederates, still consider April 1 to be induction day.

Neither at home nor at school was anything made of either

of the rivals for the title of "anniversary of Confederation." Far from knowing what day the anniversary fell on, I didn't know there was such a thing. The day had no name, as far as I can remember. The government did not officially proclaim it "Confederation Day" or something similar, as you might expect, though it was called that by confederates. Anti-confederates, when forced to refer to it, called it "induction day." The difference was that confederates saw Confederation as something we had done, while the anti-confederates saw it as something that had been done to us.

When it was getting late, after a lot of drinking had been done, and most of the children had taken up vantage points in the front room to watch the ever more entertaining grown-ups, the time came for performances. Inhibition and the ability to relate or follow such arguments as my father had been making had each declined at about the same rate. The grown-ups started shouting names of people present, nominating them, until a consensus was reached as to who should take the first turn.

Someone shouted "Art and Wayne," which was the call for a catechism, and everyone applauded. I had to be coaxed from under the piano, where I was lying on the floor beside my brothers.

My father sat on the couch, I stood facing him and he began. I had only the vaguest understanding of what followed, having memorized it more or less phonetically.

HIM: How would you assess Joey Smallwood's record since Confederation?

ME: I would demur, unless at my throat a knife was held, or at my head a gun.

HIM: Assuming one or both of these conditions to be met?

ME: I would enumerate his blunders one by one until the intervention of senility or death.

HIM: A thumbnail sketch might be extracted at less cost?

ME: The cost, though less, would still be dear.

HIM: Could you do him justice in a single sentence?

ME: Death by hanging.

When we finished, there was loud applause. After several others took their turns singing songs, it was deemed to be time for Uncle Harold to recite "Fling Out the Flag."

The Union Jack and, after 1965, the Canadian flag, stood in the corner of the school lobby, though never unfurled, as though in token, minimal observance of some provincial regulation. The only unfurled flag was Newfoundland's Pink, White and Green. It hung from the wall above the lobby doors, and it was about this flag that "Fling Out the Flag," the unofficial anthem of Newfoundland, was written in 1888 by Archbishop Howley, eighteen years before Sir Cavendish Boyle wrote his more famous "Ode to Newfoundland," which eventually became the official anthem.

The Pink, White and Green was a merging of the Pink and the Green that had taken place in 1843. The Pink, a pink flag with a green fir tree, was the flag of a group of well-established Roman Catholics in St. John's who referred to themselves as "natives" because they were born in Newfoundland and to differentiate themselves from newly arrived Irish immigrant Roman Catholics like my ancestors, whom they referred to as "The Bush-borns" and who flew a green flag with the harp of Brian Boru to represent their group.

There was a great deal of animosity between the two

groups, especially after the "natives" formed the Native Society and excluded from its membership anyone not born in New-foundland. In February of 1843, a wood-hauling contest between these two groups ended in a brawl in which, as one newspaper reported, "a good many heads were broken." The cause of the brawl was their failure to agree on which group had hauled the bigger pile of wood.

Peace between the natives and the Bush-borns was brought about by the archbishop who advised the two groups to join the Pink and Green together to form one flag, half pink, half green. They could not quite bring themselves to do that, but instead inserted a bolt of neutral white between the two colours.

As Harold did not know the music, he could only recite "Fling Out the Flag" as a poem. Glass in one hand, cigar in the other, face flushed, he launched into it without warning, and all conversation stopped.

"The Pink, the Rose of England shows,
The Green St. Patrick's emblem, bright,
While in between, the spotless sheen
Of St. Andrew's Cross displays the white.
Then hail the pink, the white, the green.
Our patriot flag long may it stand.
Our sirelands twine, their emblems trine,
To form the flag of Newfoundland!
Fling out the flag, o'er creek and cragg,
Pink, white and green, so fair, so grand.
Long may it sway o'er bight and bay,
Around the shores of Newfoundland!
Whate'er betide our 'Ocean Bride'

That nestles 'midst Atlantic's foam,
Still far and wide, we'll raise with pride
Our native flag, o'er hearth and home.
Should e'er the hand of fate demand
Some future change in our career,
We ne'er will yield, on flood or field
The Flag we honour and revere!
Fling out the flag o'er creek and cragg,
Pink, white and green, so fair, so grand.
Long may it sway o'er bight and bay,
Around the shores of Newfoundland."

"Fling Out the Flag" was greeted with applause, which had not died down when Harold launched into "The Lament for Newfoundland," published in the St. John's *Daily News* on April 1, 1949. Teary-eyed before he even started, he declaimed:

"On this day of parting, sad nostalgic thoughts arise,
Thoughts to bring the hot tears surging to the Newfoundlanders eyes,
Thoughts that bring to mind the story of the struggles of the past,
Of the men who built our island, nailed its colours to our mast.
Those who lost the fight for freedom have the greater pride this day,
Though their country's independence lies the victim of the fray.
They have kept THEIR faith untarnished, they have left THEIR honour high,

They can face the course of history with a clear and steadfast eye."

By the time Harold was finished, tears were streaming down his face. Likewise the rest of them, my father, Uncle Jim, my mother, Aunt Eva, Marg, all enjoying themselves immensely, it seemed to me.

"Well spoken, Harold, my son," my father said, his tone more consoling than laudatory. Uncle Dennis cried but was consoled by no one but his wife.

Then we sang "The Ode to Newfoundland," which most Catholics, in spite of their affection for "Fling Out the Flag," were quite fond of, for the only mention in it of religion was a non-denominational God.

"We'll have 'The Ode' now, Harold, if you please," my father said. Harold sat at the piano, and while he played, we sang.

"'As loved our fathers, so we love/Where once they stood we stand.'"

Next came a toast to Charlie and Nan, proposed by Harold. "To Charlie and Nan," they said.

My father raised his glass but did not drink. A few minutes later he put down his glass, slipped away from the party and went out to the back porch, closing the door behind him. I thought no one else had noticed until Uncle Harold, as if in mimicry of my father, took the same path through the guests as he had and went out to the porch. Looking out the kitchen window, I saw them go down the steps and walk halfway across the yard.

I went out to the porch, eased open the storm door. I watched them from behind a wooden column on the steps. My father leaned over, his hands on his thighs as if he had been sick or was about to be. Harold put one hand on my father's back and looked off into the darkness as though embarrassed. My father, I saw, was not sick but crying silently, as if something inside him had brimmed over without warning. His shoulders heaved, tears fell unchecked from his eyes onto the pavement. He shook his head from side as if he could not account for his inability to stop either of these developments. I heard him say something, heard the words "never" and "too late" and presumed that it was still the referendum that was on his mind.

"I know, my son," Uncle Harold said, "I know." "My son," he called his brother, and my father often called him that.

"You *don't* know," my father said. "Something happened. On the beach. The day I left for college. Something happened." My father said something else but I could not make it out.

"I don't think so," Harold said.

My father spoke, again inaudibly, his tone insistent as if he were repeating what he had said last and this time Harold, as if chastised, did not reply.

"Never mind," my father said. "Never mind, my son. I've had too much to drink, that's all." Across the road from Harold's house was a small lake that we called the Pond. I could not see it, but when a breeze came up, I smelled the mint weed on the shore and heard the faint lapping of the water. It was a warm summer night. I had not been up this late before, let alone outdoors at such an hour. It seemed to me that this must be the stuff of night, furtive exchanges like this between adults about things whose existence they could not acknowledge in the light of day.

I was sure that my father's sorrow did not proceed from politics. Never. Too late. I could think of nothing that would never happen, nothing for which it would forever be too late.

Finally my father straightened up and rubbed his eyes with the back of his arm, exhaled loudly, cleared his throat. He put his hands on his hips and looked up at the sky as if to signal by the scrutiny of distant stars that his thoughts had once again turned outward.

"I can't go back in now," he said. "I'll walk home."

Our house was just up the road from Harold's. Harold watched him for a while as he went down the driveway and began to make his way up the road. When Harold turned to come back, I went inside.

"THEY MIGHT BE phasing out the train," my father said, looking up from his paper one night in the fall of 1968. After Confederation, the railway had been taken over by Canadian National Railways, CNR, and now they were considering replacing the train with a less expensive fleet of buses.

Buses were an option because the first trans-island paved road had been completed in 1965. My father said the only reason people used the road was to see what pavement felt like and they would soon grow tired of it.

My father was one of many people who tried to save the train.

It was decided there would be a "trial period" from December of 1968 to May of 1969 during which both buses and trains would run across the island in a competition to see which would draw more patrons.

It was as if some feeble ghost of the referendum of 1948 had been revived. There was once again to be a kind of referendum. Patriotism would tackle pragmatism, the old Newfoundland the new Newfoundland, one last time. You could vote for the former by buying a train ticket, for the latter by buying a bus ticket. A Save the Train association was formed. There was talk it would be led by Peter Cashin. It was not.

The patriots soon had a slogan: Ride the Rails and Beat the Bus. Ads exhorting Newfoundlanders to do just that soon appeared in all the papers. The CNR countered that the price and duration of a cross-island bus ride were less than half those of the train.

My father told me that the train invoked pre-Confederate Newfoundland as nothing else could. The journey itself was as important, if not more so, than the destination. The train was designed to be lived in, not just ridden. You could not walk about on a bus as you could on a train. There was no bar on a bus. There were no tables spread with impeccably white and creased linen, no silver cutlery or crystal glasses, no one at your beck and call, happy to attend to your most eccentric needs.

The train was a reminder for my father of his first trip off the island in September of 1948. Each journey on it was a recapitulation of that one, when he had seen Newfoundland for the first time, just prior to leaving it for the first time. That trip had been for him a strange hybrid of arrival and departure, discovery and abandonment. He for some reason often brought it up when we were driving home from Ferryland, but when I asked him why, he would not tell me.

There was the circadian length of the trip. The island, as measured by the train, was almost exactly one day wide, twenty-four hours from coast to coast. One single Newfoundland-encompassing day. You departed and arrived at the same hour of the morning or the same hour of the evening. Or you did except when there were blockages along the line, when huge snowdrifts arced across the tracks and the train was stalled for days, as happened regularly on a northwest section of the line called the Gaff Topsails where, as the Pragmatists pointed out, it was not unusual for a passenger-filled train to be stranded for days, twenty unwalkable miles from the nearest settlement. The length of one memorable train trip had been more lunar than circadian, a group of travellers stalled in a train on the Gaff Topsails for twenty-six days. About a hundred times as many Newfoundlanders as it was possible for the train to hold claimed to have been on that run.

On the train you travelled by night, and the night always found you in the "core," as my father called it, in the wild, unsettled middle of the island as far inland as you could go except on foot. The train was a moving hotel and the whole of Newfoundland went by outside your window; it was a restaurant on wheels with an ever-changing view, one kind of landscape giving way to another as if the island were composed of many countries. The dining and sleeping accommodations were, as trains go, luxurious.

What percentage of the train supporters had voted against Confederation in 1948 is impossible to say, but my father said that a large majority had. Unfortunately for them, it was announced before the "trial period" even started that according to a poll, Newfoundlanders preferred the bus to the train by five to one. Before the campaign to save it got off the ground, the train was doomed. The faster, cheaper buses that were setting out from St. John's each morning were packed, while whole train cars that left from Riverhead Station were empty, pulled pointlessly along behind the few that were occupied. The loss of the train would be yet another of the foul fruits of

Confederation. But father and the others clung to the notion
that as soon as the novelty of the bus wore off, and as soon as
the weather softened in the spring and there was no longer any
possibility of being stranded on the tracks, the train would make
up the gap. Or, as a compromise, the government would decide
to run the train only from May to November.

There was talk for a while that all the Johnstons and
the Everards would book passage on a final Christmas run
the day after Boxing Day, from St. John's to Port aux Basques
and back. My father and Harold pitched it to the others, and
there was talk of a grand expedition. But interest in the trip
soon fell off when it was discovered how expensive it would
be. The only such group trip across the island that we could
have afforded would have been by bus. My older brothers
were of an age when to travel with one's parents was no longer
an adventure. If not all of us were going, my mother could
not go. Eva and Jim bowed out. Marg would not go unless
my mother did. The Everards had never been that interested.
The number of travellers dwindled gradually until there were
just my father and me and Harold left, and then Harold had to
cancel out because of work. That left only ten-year-old me and
my father.

We started out from St. John's just after sunrise on
December 27, 1968. There was no snow on the east coast. The
new highway roughly shadowed the railway tracks except for
taking the short and easy way around most obstacles, and except
for the elevated Gaff Topsails stretch, which the highway avoid-
ed altogether, instead forking up to Springdale on the coast,
then down southwest again, more or less meeting up with the
train tracks at Deer Lake.

We were sometimes able to see the highway from the train, and once, not far outside of St. John's, we ran all but side by side with one of the Roadcruiser buses. I had been surprised at Riverhead Station to see how small the buses were. It was hard to imagine them posing any threat to the train, which stretched as far as I could see, the initials CNR repeated on each car until they became an indecipherable white blur.

But I found myself now treacherously rooting for that single silver bus. I was impressed by how much faster it was moving than we were. The bus looked like a sleek, wingless plane and, in comparison with the many-sectioned train, seemed so heroically singular, so self-sufficient. The highway itself seemed a marvel to me, its sides clear-cut of trees and bush, as did the strange sight of pavement in the woods, with those reassuringly artificial white lines down the middle that somehow made the wilderness less desolate. The weathered, wooden train, the wooden, black-tarred ties, the rusting rails, the ancient railway bed along which trees had grown to full height since the line went through in 1898, the once-pink granite gravel now washed grey with age all seemed to blend in with the landscape, an unobtrusiveness that to some was one of its merits, though it did not seem so to me.

We remained side by side with the bus only because of the train's length. People, my father not among them, crowded one side of the train to see it. Children stuck out their tongues at it, though what effect this had on its driver or its occupants we couldn't tell, for its windows were tinted.

The railway and the road diverged, and the bus passed from view for several minutes, then was distantly visible, far ahead and to the right of us, turning sharply away from the railway track as if it were headed across a different island than we were, a more modern, train-excluding island. After it next passed from view, we did not see that bus again, though we came to within yards of the highway many times.

It was on this train trip that I finally crossed the Isthmus of Avalon. For a time on the isthmus, as when we drove in the car until forced back by the fog, we could see the ocean on either side. Then we plunged into the river of fog, and I was awed by the certainty that this time we would not turn round but would come out the other side, as if the train could do what our little car could not. We rumbled through the fog. I pressed my face to the window, just able to make out vague shapes and colours.

And then suddenly we hurtled out of Avalon into the mundane world. I imagined the view of someone watching from trackside as more and more of the train emerged from the tunnel of fog, some of it out, some of it still inside, my imaginary spectator wondering if the train would ever end, then seeing the car with me inside, my face pressed to the glass, looking for the first time on this the origin of grievous wounds.

It looked exactly like Avalon, but I had expected it would, had prepared myself for this illusion and was almost able to convince myself that we were now sub-Avalon, pre-Avalon, post-Avalon, lapsed in some way all the more sinister for being imperceptible. We were in the land of the baymen now, the land of the bush-borns.

For a while we travelled parallel to the highway again. Cars overtook us with embarrassing ease. Then a Roadcruiser bus.

"Look," my father said, loud enough for the whole car to hear, "it's that bloody bus again."

"Not the same one," a man sitting several seats ahead of us said, remaining face forward so that all we could see of him was the back of his head, a starched shirt collar, the shoulders of an impeccable new black suit. "That one left Riverhead two hours after we did. Caught up with us already."

"It looks like a lunch bucket on wheels," my father said, and many people let out snorts of derision.

"It may not look like much," the man said, "but it gets you where you want to go faster than this train does."

"Does it, now?" my father said. "Well, what are you doing on the train if you love the bus so much?"

"Never said I loved the bus," the man said, still not turning round. "But we might as well face facts —"

A collective groan cut the man short. The need to "face facts" was the pro-bus argument, and they had heard it all before. My father asked the man again what he was doing on the train if he loved the bus so much.

"Never said I loved the bus," the man said, as if he was implacably determined not to have words put in his mouth. "Taking one last ride for old times' sake, like everybody else. We might just as well face facts —"

The woman beside him, whom I presumed was his wife, gave him a now-don't-go-starting-something nudge with her shoulder. The man straightened up as if in silent defiance of her warning.

"Why might we just as well face facts?" my father said. "Could you tell me that? Why might we just as well face facts? If we all faced facts, there'd be no one left in Newfoundland. There's nothing in the facts to keep us here."

I knew from his tone of voice and his expression that he

was one provocation away from launching into an attack on Joey Smallwood, the fixed referendum and Confederation. I half-hoped, half-dreaded, that the man would say something else. There was a nervous silence in the car.

"We're a country of fact-facing bus-boomers," my father said, grinning, looking out the window.

"A province," the fact-facing bus-boomer said. "We're a province now, not a country. Never were a country, really. If you know your history." I heard in his voice a politeness that was meant to be transparently insincere, patronizing, the tone of someone who held in reserve a trump card he need never play. I could just see it. A riot on the train fought over a matter decided twenty years ago.

"I know *my* history," my father said. "A province of progress, is that what we are?" "A province of progress" was one of Joey's latest slogans.

"Better than a backward country," the fact-facing bus-boomer said. It was all there now, just beneath the surface. His continuing to face forward while he spoke, showing us nothing but the back of his head was clearly getting to my father. He had no idea what my father looked like, nor did he care to know, the back of his head seemed to say.

"Is this what we'll have to listen to, from here to Port aux Basques," my father said, "a fact-facing, bus-booming, arse-kissing civil servant?" My father all but spat out the last two words as if thereby expressing his distaste for his own occupation with the federal Fisheries department and ridding himself of the self-contempt he had to live with every day.

"One last look for old times' sake," my father said. "Tell me, if your mother was going under for the third time, would

you take one last look for old times' sake? What am I saying
— of course you would."

I was sure the man would turn around now, but he didn't.
A purser whose CNR uniform lent him an authority that belied
his skinny, almost puny frame and who must have heard my
father came halfway up the stairs of the observation car, just
to show himself, a tacit reminder that no troublemaking would
be tolerated.

My father looked at the man across the aisle from us and
both of them smiled and looked at the fact-facing bus-boomer,
the back of whose neck was now a livid red. His wife was grip-
ping his upper arm with both her hands, her head bobbing
emphatically as if she were urgently whispering to him.

It was probably no coincidence that just before the train
stopped at Gambo, the birthplace of Joey Smallwood, the bus-
boomer and his wife got up and left the observation car, which
they were able to do without turning round to face my father,
the stairway that led down below being several rows in front of
them. We only saw them briefly in profile as they went quickly down the steps. All I remember of them is that both were
blushing so that they looked as if through years of marriage they
had developed perfectly compatible complexions.

"We might as well face facts." That was not just the argument for the bus. It had been the argument for Confederation.
The confederates hadn't argued for Canada per se because most
Newfoundlanders knew nothing more about Canada than what
little they had heard from Canadian servicemen stationed in St.
John's throughout the war. There had been far more Americans
stationed there, a friendly occupation force that had poured
money into Newfoundland, building military installations that

had yet to be shut down. Wartime was looked back on by Newfoundlanders as the American era, years when they saw firsthand the swaggering largesse of the country to which thousands of their relatives had gone in search of jobs.

On the siding at Gambo, my father did not once look out the window. But neither did Gambo inspire him to hold forth as I thought it would. Perhaps if the bus-boomer had stayed . . .

My father sat in silence, engrossed, or pretending to be, in a book he'd brought along. Brooding, more likely. I had thought that by leaving, the bus-boomer had admitted defeat. But now I saw that he had not, that he had left because he had no need to argue: for the bus, for Smallwood, for Confederation, for anything. It was on this my father was brooding, on the smirk implicit in the man's every word.

We won, we won and nothing you can say can change that fact, and nothing makes victory sweeter than the enduring bitterness of men like you. That was the meaning of their disdainful march from the observation car.

Sometime in the afternoon, I dozed off and did not wake up until we were approaching the Gaff Topsails, a steep-sloped tract of wilderness, the highest point on the line and the place where delays were most likely in the winter when the tracks were blocked by snow. The tracks along the Topsails were not only elevated but flat, so even when it wasn't snowing all that was needed to bury the tracks was wind, which blew into drifts snow that was already on the ground.

On this day, the tracks were open, but barely. The previous train had cut a trench between snow walls, which got higher as we moved into the Topsails until we could see nothing from either side of the train except sheer cliffs of snow mere inches from the windows. After that, even in the observation car, we could only tell how much deeper the trench was getting by how much darker it became in the train, for snow drifted across the top of the trench, blocking out the sky.

Finally, the train began to slow down. "Snow on the tracks," my father said. We could not see the snow on the tracks, but we soon felt the train nudge into it. We jolted forward slightly in our seats. Once the cowcatcher had edged into the snowdrift, the engineer increased the throttle. A great grinding noise began from the front of the train and moved down the length of it; soon the floor of our car was vibrating. We moved along at two or three miles an hour at most, though the locomotive roared as if we were going at full speed.

The train continued in this fashion for a while, then slowed more as we began to go upgrade. We made excruciatingly suspenseful progress for about three miles, the passengers urging the train on, knowing that if we stalled we might be stranded for days. We laughed and rocked forward in our seats as if to coax the locomotive one more inch, and then one more until at last we felt it make the crest and a great cheer went up.

Going downgrade was much easier, though we could not go at regular speed, for there were drifts across the tracks that might have derailed us had we crashed through them too fast. Every so often, as we hit one, we lurched forward in our seats, everyone shouting "Whoa!" and watching as the exploding snow went flying past our windows.

In one way, we were crossing Newfoundland at the worst possible time, during the season of least light, a week past the day of least light. About half of the island we didn't see at all,

and some of it we saw at twilight, from four to six in the afternoon, from six to eight in the morning. But you hadn't really
seen Newfoundland, my father had told me before we set out,
until you had seen it in winter from the train.

In the course of our journey westward, we saw the sun
rise and set and rise again. The journey began and ended at sunrise. We went from light to dark to light again. And regardless
of what time of year it was, we would have travelled through
some part of the core in darkness. The core was the vast basin
that lay within the bowl of the coastal mountains beyond which,
before the train, almost no one had set foot. And you always
passed through the core of the core in the middle of the night
whether you travelled in June or in December.

It was easy to imagine, impossible not to, that the core
was always dark, that on this middle wilderness the sun *never*
rose and the most it ever had by way of light it got on those
rare nights when the sky was clear and the moon was full.

We were surrounded from without by a wilderness of
water and from within by one of land, an expansive assertion
of land about which, before the train went through, next to
nothing was known, had been seen by no one, not even by aboriginals who lived within a few miles of the coast, no one except
a few people such as William Cormack. My father, who loved
planting misconceptions in my head, told me the core was
named after Cormack.

To prepare for our trip, I had read Cormack's account of
his walk across the island. In 1822, at the age of twenty-six, he
walked from Trinity Bay on the east coast to Bay St. George
on the west coast. He set out on September 5, accompanied
by a Micmac named Joe Sylvester, and completed his walk on

November 4, then wrote his *Narrative of a Journey Across the Island of Newfoundland, the Only One Ever Performed by a European.* By European, he meant someone of European descent, for Cormack, though Old World educated, was New World born, having grown up in St. John's and gone to university in Scotland.

He was a solitary soul who before setting out wrote that it was a comfort to him to know that "no one would be injured by my annihilation." It seemed a heart-rendingly pathetic thing to say about yourself. I could not imagine a man more profoundly alone than the one who had written that.

He called the core the Terra Incognita, the unknown land. Before Cormack's walk, there were fantastic stories about its inhabitants, stories about a race of giant aboriginals and strange animals of a sort that lived nowhere else on earth but Newfoundland.

Cormack, though he discovered no such marvels, found most of what he saw beyond his powers of description. "In vain were associations," he wrote, "in vain did the eyes wander for the cattle, the cottage and the flocks." This landscape for which he searched in vain was not even that of *coastal* Newfoundland but that of England, or more precisely the England of books, which formed his image of "home." All Cormack could do was catalogue what he saw. He attempted an exhaustive geological and botanical catalogue, recording in his journal every rock and form of plant life, half his journal consisting of italicized Latin.

To keep himself sane, to make the landscape seem less alien, to remind himself that the outside world still existed and that he would return to it someday, Cormack named lakes and mountains after people he had gone to school with, old college mates, old teachers. Some of what he had seen was gone now, such as the "dense, unbroken pine, an ocean of undulating forest" that covered the first twenty miles of his trip. Cormack had seen the "pine-clad hills" of which Boyle wrote in "The Ode to Newfoundland," but most of the pine was gone, cut down or burnt.

In the latter part of his walk, Cormack had wound up delirious, alternating between despair of ever reaching his destination and delusions of invincibility, during which he hoped the walk would last forever. He had stood atop some knob of rock and caught what he thought was his first sight of the Gulf of St. Lawrence, the western sea of Newfoundland, and told Joe Sylvester that they would not stop walking until they reached it, which he was sure they could do within a day.

A week later they made it to the shore — not of the Gulf but of a lake the size of a small sea. They had encountered many lakes, and rather than walk around them, they sailed across on makeshift rafts, weaving spruce boughs into sails, the two of them so exhausted they would rather risk drowning than add ten or twenty miles to their walk. They sat for hours on the shores of lakes, waiting for an east wind, which is not generally a good wind for sailing since it almost always brings bad weather, but they cared only that the wind was headed for the west as they were. They put out onto the lakes on their rafts and let the wind blow them to the other side.

They clung to or lashed themselves to the trunks of their spruce-tree masts, rising and falling on the waves that washed over them and their supplies, Sylvester screaming in the middle of each crossing that Cormack would never again coax him across a lake in such a manner. They left a trail of these little spruce-bough sail rafts behind them on the shores of lakes across the width of Newfoundland.

When they finally did sight the real sea, they kept walking after dark, Cormack running blindly through the woods, sliding down the sides of the Lewis Hills. They arrived at Bay St. George at one in the morning, able only to hear the Gulf, whose limitless expanse Cormack had so looked forward to surveying with triumph. He had thought they would reach the coast by sunrise but this time had overestimated the distance. There was nothing at the end of their journey but darkness, out into which Cormack threw beach rocks and heard but did not see the splash they made.

That was what I remembered best from the narrative — Cormack and his mystified Micmac guide sliding down the west-coast hills in the middle of the night, by doing which, he said, "We found ourselves with whole bones but many bruises." The next day he reflected in his notebook: "All was now, however, accomplished, and I hailed the glance of the sea as home and as the parent of everything dear."

Landsman though he was, he was as happy to see the ocean as Cabot had been to sight land. Cabot's voyage from Dorset in England to Cape Bonavista in Newfoundland had taken thirty-five days. Cormack's walk had taken sixty. Though he lived to the age of seventy-two, he undertook no further such expeditions and never did fully recover from that one.

We passed through a long stretch where there was more water than land, where more of the land lay underwater than did not, though it was all fresh water, rivers, pools, ponds, lakes. It was as if some great reservoir was slowly drying up, strands of bog and rock appearing in what had been the reservoir's more shallow parts. The rail line zigzagged across this stretch, following the land unless a body of water was sufficiently narrow that a trestle could be built across it. There was nothing as far as the eye could see in any direction but flat white frozen lakes and, barely distinguishable from them by the unevenness of their terrain and the occasional dark gash of green, the bogs and barrens, with here and there a tolt that ten thousand years ago had been an island rising from the water like some observation tower.

Then we passed into a landscape that was like a lake bed from which the water had receded altogether, an expansive, flat-bottomed bed of a lake that looked as though it had been uniformly three feet deep, nothing but rubble and jagged shards of granite.

And this became the pattern. Every so often, a new, entirely different, geography would assert itself. We came upon a desert of black peat bog on which there was no snow, though there was snow all around it, as if a deluge of water ten miles wide had splashed down. Here and there the peat bog had collapsed of its own weight, its soggy crust caved in to form a great crater of peat, a black bog hole that was warmer than the air so that steam issued up from it like smoke. You could tell from these peat pits that underneath its topmost layer, the whole bog was like this, a steaming black muck too loose to support the roots of even the smallest of trees.

Each part made you forget the others existed. In the middle of each landscape, you couldn't help thinking that it stretched endlessly in all directions, that this was the island's prevailing terrain and all else was anomalous.

My father had wanted me to see all this. How much land there was, how like a country Newfoundland was in its dimensions and variousness. In the days leading up to the trip, I had many times asked him, "How big is Newfoundland?" Using the map on the kitchen wall, he tried to make me understand how big it was, tried to give me some sense of how much more of it there was than I had seen so far in our drives around the bay.

"We're here," my father said, pointing at the tiny star that stood for St. John's. "Now last Sunday, when we went out for our drive, we went this far." He moved his finger in a circle about an inch across. Then he moved his hand slowly over the rest of the map. The paper crackled beneath his fingers. "Newfoundland is this much bigger than that," he said, making the motion with his hand again. "All this is Newfoundland, but it's not all like St. John's. Almost all of it is empty. No one lives there. No one's ever seen most of it."

It was an island, yes, but I had been fooled by that fact into thinking of the land as an insignificant interruption of a sea so huge that by comparison the land did not exist. There were regions of it that even the train did not come near, peninsulas along which not even branch lines had been built, the Great Northern Peninsula for instance, along the two-hundred-mile stretch of which there was neither road nor railway. It had taken the robust Cormack those sixty days of continuous walking to reach the west coast, and he had not come within a hundred miles of the Great Northern Peninsula.

The point of this journey was to get me away from the sea so that when I went back to living within two miles of it, I would know the land was there, land whose capacity to inspire wonder in all those who beheld it was in no way diminished by its being coloured the colour of Canada on maps.

How many of the outporters who had voted for Confederation, my father asked me, had had any sense of the land, the scope and shape of it, the massive fact of it? Fishermen went far enough from shore to see some of the land assuming shapes and lines, a series of capes or a small peninsula, perhaps, with headlands soon fading to a blue blur on either side, the amorphous, nebulous elsewhere whose existence was less real to them than that of the moon or the sun. They had conceived of Newfoundland as a ribbon of rock, a coast without a core, a rim with water outside and nothing, a void, inside. And stranded on this thin rim they lived, the Terra Incognita at their backs and the sea before them. For many of them, Newfoundland had not even been a coast but a discrete shard of rock, their own little cove or bay, inlet or island. They had had no idea when they cast their votes what they were voting for or what they were renouncing. They had not known there was a country, for they had never seen it or even spoken to anyone who had. What lay beyond the farthest limits of their travels and their eyesight was just a rumour, a region of fancy and conjecture. And what was true of space was true of time. What was true of geography was true of history. In how many homes or even classrooms was there a copy of Prowse's *History of Newfoundland*? Time was local, personal and even then less enduring than their experience of space, the circumscribed geography of "home." Smallwood had said that for him the main purpose of Confederation was to undo this isolation, but of course it only made it worse. For if people could not conceive of the whole of Newfoundland, how could they form any conception of a place the size of Canada?

When it was very late and the car was dark and almost empty and most of those still in it were asleep, I looked out the window at what, at that hour, I could see of Newfoundland, dark shapes of hills and trees, a glimpse, when the moon was out, of distant ice-caught ponds. The towns in the interior, though they tended to be larger than the coastal fishing towns, each one depending on some single industry like mining or pulp and paper, were few and far between. These were new towns, settlements of this century, in some cases post-confederate, lived in by people who had moved in from the coast or from small islands off the coast. But even in the core there were a few small, unaccountably located towns a hundred miles apart, nothing more than clumps of houses really, all with their porch lights on, but otherwise unlit, occupied by people who, though it passed by every night, rarely saw or even heard the train. People left over from towns built up round industries of Smallwood's that had already failed.

From Corner Brook, we followed the Long Range Mountains southwest to Stephenville Crossing, going downstream along the black, cliff-channelled Humber River. Sometime early in the morning, I fell asleep again and did not wake until the sun was up. Someone said we were thirty miles from Port aux Basques.

Until the ride back from Port aux Basques, we had a day to kill. There was not much more to do in Port aux Basques, especially without a car, than watch the ferries come and go. That is what we did, after we spent the night in the Holiday Inn that had been built for Come Home Year and had not been filled to capacity since.

Port aux Basques harbour had been dredged and redredged and hacked out of rock to accommodate the huge Gulf ferries after 1949. It looked like a quarry at high tide and at low tide like a reservoir that had been all but drained of water, the high waterline ringing the harbour basin, a white salt stain on the rocks, strands of kelp hanging down from it into the water like dark green climbing ropes.

My father pointed out to me an island, on the leeward side of which, he said, Basque fishermen after whom the town was named used to lie in wait in their boats for schools of whales. He told me of the sealing vessel *Southern Cross*, which in April of 1914, while trying to make it back from the ice floes laden down with seventeen thousand whitecoat baby seals, sank with the loss of 170 men. No trace of her or her crew was ever found, despite the fact that she got near enough to home to be spotted momentarily by the telegrapher at Port aux Basques. The *Southern Cross* that almost made it and yet no trace of which was found. What a typically Newfoundland disaster that seemed to be, the ship that almost made it but that didn't for reasons no one was able to explain.

Everything ended or, depending on your point of view, began in Port aux Basques: the highway, the railway, the Gulf run. In between the sudden, short-lived euphoria of arrivals and departures, the place was desolately empty. The port was for leaving and arriving, not for staying in. No one who could help it, no one who knew boredom when they saw it coming, spent the night in Port aux Basques.

My father found the whole concept of the car ferry hilarious, cars driving into and out of the holds of boats. The Gulf run from Argentia, near St. John's, had only recently begun and he had yet to go there, so this was a first for him, as was everything for me.

We watched a ferry arrive, churning up half the harbour, turning the green water white as it described a slow circle, then backing up to the dock and dropping its massive metal door, which doubled as a ramp.

"It's like the troop ships at Normandy," my father said. The port was a beachhead for tourists who poured off the troop-ship-like ferries in cars and trailers and transport trucks. Cars driven by motorists who you could not help thinking had been behind the wheel since the ferry left North Sydney and seemed to know exactly where to go sped off. They left Newfoundland the same way, like an invasion force withdrawing with almost comic haste, its mission either accomplished or abandoned as hopeless. The whole thing seemed portentous of some mass evacuation.

We watched as hundreds of cars assembled on a parking lot the size of several football fields waiting to drive onto the Gulf ferry. Some had out-of-province licence plates — Canadian, American — but most bore the plates of Newfoundland.

Every day of the summers since the road went through in '65, hundreds of Newfoundlanders drove to Port aux Basques, took the ferry to the mainland, then spent their vacations enjoying the previously unheard of luxury of endless driving, endless space. The number of car owners increased threefold after 1965. Air travel was still, for most people, too expensive or too exotic. With the road, and without the train, Newfoundland was suddenly transformed from a country where it was pointless to have a car to a country where you could not get by without one. "Going for drives" became the rage, the way it had in other parts of the world in the 1920s.

Several lanes were reserved for transport trucks, which lined up in convoys and were always the first on and the first off any ferry. I had heard there was not enough room on many parts of the highway for two transport trucks to pass without one relieving the other of its sideview mirror. Only a few people boarded the ferry the old-fashioned way, walking on, some bus passengers, some backpacking students who had hitchhiked across the island. "The boat used to dock side-on," my father said scornfully, "not stern-on like that. There used to be a gangplank."

Every day for years these melodramas of departure and arrival had been going on without my knowledge. I had been nowhere. I had never been this far west before. On the island. In the world. Children half my age looked out at me from the windows of the cars that went on board the ferry, travel complacent five-year-olds to whom I was sure my unworldliness was obvious.

I decided that when I left the island for the first time, it would be by boat. It would be appropriate, the first time, to watch the land slowly fade from view. I looked out to where the ferry was headed, but there was no more sign of land than there was when you looked out to sea from the Gaze at Ferryland.

Only according to the map was Canada closer than Ireland and England. Places I had never been and could not see were all impossibly far away, nebulously elsewhere. My father saw me looking wonder-struck. It must have occurred to him that this was the first time I had ever set eyes on the Gulf of St. Lawrence. "It looks just the same on the other side," he said. "For a while, anyway."

I nodded as if I had assumed this to be the case. But I did not really believe it. Crossing the stream of fog on the isthmus of Avalon was momentous enough for now. This other crossing I was contemplating I could not imagine. The other side of *this* Gulf was remoter than the moon, on which men had just landed and which I had seen with my own eyes countless times. Only on TV and in photographs had I ever seen the world alleged to exist beyond the shores of Newfoundland. I had read about it in books, but any book not set in Newfoundland was to me a work of fiction. Anywhere but Newfoundland was to me as fabled a place as the New World must have been to Cabot or Columbus.

"We should drive here sometime, Dad," I said. "All of us. Or we could leave from Argentia. Take the ferry across. On your holidays."

"Sure," he said. "Sure, we'll do that soon."

A man told my father that some people had taken the bus from St. John's to Port aux Basques so they could take the train back to St. John's. And people from Port aux Basques and from other places between there and St. John's planned to take the train to St. John's, then go home by bus. My father could not understand this. You were either for the bus or for the train. You could not have it both ways.

"They're all a crowd of fact-facing bus-boomers," my father said.

There were not many purists like us who boarded the train that morning, but what few there were were easy to spot because of how travel-weary they looked, about to begin their second crossing of Newfoundland in two days.

It was clear from the outset that there would be no sleeping on this trip. Nor was anyone likely to complain about the noise. It was as if invitations had been sent out to a train-borne talent contest.

Two old men in coveralls got on board wearing accordions but otherwise without luggage. A fiddler warmed up on the platform. "Or at least I hope he's warming up," my father said. He wondered if it was all some sort of celebration got up by the government.

A man boarded with a set of spoons hanging from his belt. Another fellow step-danced as if to a tune that no one else could hear, standing ramrod straight, arms rigidly at his sides, moving about among the people on the platform who paid him a disconcerting lack of attention. He was very trim, well-dressed except he had no jacket, just a shirt and vest and slacks and gleaming black shoes. My father said he was either per-forming some sort of send-off for the train or was completely mad. Luggage was generally scarce. Some people carried noth-ing but bottles of rum tokenly disguised in paper bags. Others toted impossible-to-disguise cases of beer.

"We couldn't save her, so we might as well give her a proper send-off," one beer-laden man said, as if to disarm the conductor as he handed him his ticket. Drinking was permitted almost everywhere, in the observation car, the smoking car, the dining car, coach.

"I wouldn't want to have your head this time tomorrow," the conductor said, shaking his own head but grinning. I had seen two bottles of Royal Reserve rye whisky in my father's suitcase.

We stowed our luggage in our berth, then went where everyone else was going, to the observation car. Most of the people who had got on board did not have berths. They were travelling coach, probably unable to afford a berth but in any case with no need for one on this occasion, for they had no intention of even spending time by themselves, let alone sleeping.

The purser was cheered when he broke out two bottles of Champagne. On every run from now until the last one in the spring, my father said, there would be Champagne. A token of mollification. I foresaw a long twenty-four hours for children and other non-drinkers. There were not many children. There would be little for me to do but watch the grown-ups.

The step dancer eventually got on the train. Now that he had stopped dancing, people took notice of him and called him by name, Walter.

"Not much room to scuff in here, Walter," one man said.

"He don't need much room," a woman said. Walter said nothing, just smiled, as if in humble acknowledgment of fame. Nor did it seem that anyone expected him to speak.

The accordionists came up the steps to the observation car. They were so alike that they must have been brothers. They began to play, making a sound like a hundred car horns blowing in raucous celebration of a wedding. No one else seemed to mind. No one paid much attention to the scenery or the blue sky and white clouds visible through the glass roof. A singalong was soon under way, of Newfoundland songs, though there was not a railway song among them or one in which the word "train" was even mentioned.

I kept my eye on Walter. He sat near the circular staircase that led up to the observation car, beside the accordionists. He did not move a muscle. There was nothing to indicate that he was keeping time with the music or even remotely aware of his surroundings. Then he stood up and, as if in a trance, began to dance as he had on the platform, as if driven to do so by some force he was helpless to resist, though he was so stiff that all of him except his feet did seem to be resisting. He looked nonplussed but composed, as if, though it was a long-standing mystery to him why his feet behaved the way they did, he knew he had no choice but to wait for them to stop. He went up and down between the aisle while everyone clapped along.

Soon others were dancing, as many as the limited space would permit. Glasses were abandoned, temporarily or not, all over the place. I poured the contents of a couple into an almost-empty Coke bottle and proceeded to get drunk for the first time in my life. My father saw what I was up to but said nothing. His main concern was not that I was drinking but that my mother not find out.

Having downed most of the contents of my Coke bottle at the rate that I normally consumed Coke, I felt as though I might be sick. I kept perfectly still, concentrating on not being sick, convinced that unless everyone around me kept perfectly still and concentrated on my not becoming sick, I was doomed.

Luckily for me, sleep came first. I passed out in a chair by the window. When I woke up hours later, the party, accordion driven, was still going strong. People looked out the windows, but only to see where we were, to revel in how much of the journey still remained. Time was being measured solely in terms of space. The party would last for 638 miles, and so far we had travelled only 160.

A mummers' troupe was on the train, though we in the observation car did not realize this until we heard a voice from the bottom of the stairs say "Mummers allowed in?" and another "Any Christmas here?"

"*Mummers!*" someone shouted.

From below the observation car, there was an explosion of sound from which we had not even begun to recover when there came climbing up the stairs like some invasion force a troupe of mummers, all wearing costumes that disguised not only their identities but their genders, the lead one holding above his/her head with both hands a suitcase-size radio that was cranked up to what must have been full volume and playing some sort of frenzied raucous jig.

The other mummers, perhaps ten or twelve of them, fell in behind him/her single file, half-jogging, half-shaking, each using to deafening effect some sort of noisemaker — one was playing on his/her hip a set of spoons, another had what looked something like but wasn't quite a tambourine, another had on his/her arm a shield-like drum and was beating it with both ends of what appeared to be a pepper grinder; another was not so much playing as blowing into a mouth organ in a way that sounded like the random honking of a flock of geese; another was rattling on the end of a stick or whip what was supposed to be, and for all I know may well have been, a bladder full of peas.

The noise of their instruments combined with that blasting from the radio to make such a din that people from the rest of the train came up to see what was going on.

"Oh look, it's the mummers," one of the women said and ran back down the stairs, presumably to spread the news.

Though I doubted there was anyone on the train who would have recognized them, the mummers spoke ingressively — that is, while breathing in — as mummers visiting the houses of people they knew did in order to disguise their voices. Their every word was a hoarse croaking gasping inhalation.

I had never seen mummers before. There hadn't been much mummering done in or around St. John's for a long time. It had been outlawed there since the 1860s, as it had been on the entire Avalon Peninsula, largely because one Isaac Mercer had been set upon and murdered by a troupe of mummers on December 28, 1860, in Bay Roberts, a town not far from St. John's.

Because mummers went from house to house bumming booze or wandered with bottles in hand through the streets, becoming progressively more drunk and less inhibited, their jaunts sometimes ended in fistfights. And mummering was in some places a time-honoured way of getting revenge for past grievances by using the disguise to beat the living daylights out of enemies. Religious rivals went at each other, Catholics preying on Protestants and vice versa.

There had been plenty of mummering in Ferryland when my father was growing up, despite the law that had been passed against it and despite the parish priest's condemnation. The priest, every Christmas, denounced mummering as blasphemous, pornographic and obscene. Mummers were depraved, he said. While dancing with mummers, people would "feel them up" to determine what sex they were. In which case, he said, you not only had men groping women and vice versa, but men groping men and women groping women. And this was a tradition people thought was worth reviving? "Have nothing to do with mummering," he said.

The members of this troupe wore homemade masks, veils of lace or net curtains, or pillowcases or stockings pulled tightly over their faces, tied at the throat with twine. Some had wigs and false beards, and what little that showed of their faces was painted black.

There was a mummer with a middle leg so long that it dragged the ground, an opaque stocking stuffed with socks that he/she kept stepping on and tripping.

There was a "Horse-chops" too, who was "riding" a hobby-horse made of a stick with the figure of a horse's head on top, a head that had moveable jaws with nails for teeth that he/she snapped at people's noses, ingressively laughing when they pulled back, half-terrified, half-amused.

They sang ingressively an old song that the accordion brothers knew. It was, I found out later, called, "The Terra Novean Exile's Song": "How oft some of us here tonight/Have seen the mummers out/As thro' the fields by pale moon light/They came with merry shout/In costumes quaint with mask or paint."

Eventually, the lead mummer held out a hand to a woman who without the least hesitation accepted, and the two of them, arms linked, began what was obviously not the first such dance for either of them. The other mummers followed suit.

I was approached by a mummer wearing a red dress with black polka dots over green slacks tucked into knee-high rubber boots; for a mask it wore a pillow slip, with eyeholes but no mouth, tied at the neck with green twine, a pair of woollen mitts, a large blue floppy hat with a fringe of flowers. There was so much padding underneath the dress I couldn't have come within a hundred pounds of guessing the person's weight, and over the dress was an enormous stuffed bra and an equally enormous rosette-embroidered pair of panties. "Give us a dance?" I shook my head, which ached. I felt queasy. I was hung over, though I didn't know it.

I knew it was supposed to be all in fun, but there was something about mummering itself I didn't like, something I would not have liked had I been living in a time when mummering was commonplace. Partly it was the mummers themselves; there was something of the bully about them. It was an uneasy feeling, to be forced to take part in something so one-sided, to be at such a disadvantage — the mummers were anonymous, uninhibited, aggressive, because you couldn't see their faces, while there you were for all to see.

The mummer wearing the middle leg that hung down almost to the floor danced over to my father, that leg lewdly swinging, and held out an arm to him. Smiling and trying not to look the least bit disconcerted, he shook his head. It soon became clear, however, that refusal was unacceptable. The mummer grabbed his middle leg with both hands and, raising it, made as if to knight my father with it, laying it first on one shoulder, then the other.

"I wants a dance," he/she said ingressively. "What's the matter? Townies don't dance?"

"I'm no townie," my father said. "What's your name?"

"It's not time yet for guessin' names," the mummer said. "It's time to dance," and this time with the middle leg bopped my father on the head.

"I'm not in the mood for dancing," my father said. "You lot aren't planning to keep this up all the way to the other side of the country, are you?"

The mummer put his face to within inches of my father's and, speaking ingressively, said, "It's not a country, it's a province. It never was a country. If you know your history."

My father made a lunge for him, but several other mummers

intervened and hustled away the one who by his words had revealed himself to be the fact-facing bus-boomer.

"Downstairs," one of them said ingressively. "We're going downstairs now. Time to visit somewhere else. Somewhere we'll be more welcome." The mummers, accompanied by the makeshift band and many of the occupants of the observation car, departed as abruptly as they had arrived, though for a long time afterwards we could still hear them down below.

My father sat brooding again, looking out the window for a while. It had been comical, his lunging for the middle-leg-wearing fact-facing bus-boomer, though it did not seem so now. Those passengers still in the car darted a glance at him from time to time.

He got up and told me to stay put until he got back — he was going to take a short nap in our berth. I thought he might be going off in search of the fact-facing bus-boomer, but he went the other way. We never saw the bus-boomer, mummered up or otherwise, again.

My father came back about an hour later and rejoined me in the seat. "Were you going to beat him up?" I said.

My father laughed. His mood was much improved and I could tell why just from looking at him.

"No," he said, "I wasn't going to beat him up." But he laughed as if he was picturing the fact-facing, bus-booming mummer thrashed, his costume in a state of extreme dishevelment.

When night came, he fell silent again, staring out into the darkness. We had something to eat in the dining car, then went back to our berth.

I climbed into bed. He turned off the light and sat by the window, facing me, a glass in one hand that he rested on his leg. "You go to sleep," he said. "I'll wake you when the sun comes up and we'll have breakfast in the dining car. Don't tell your mother what happened, all right?"

I nodded. "Where will we be when the sun comes up?" I said.

He took his schedule from his pocket and squinted at it in the darkness. "Whitbourne Junction," he said.

"Tell me a ghost story," I said.

He shook his head. "You'll have bad dreams."

"No I won't," I said.

He told me about the *Great Eastern*. The first underwater transatlantic telegraph cable had been brought ashore at Heart's Content, Newfoundland, on July 27, 1866. For the purpose of laying the cable between Valenica, Ireland and Heart's Content, a telegraph company owner named Cyrus Field had purchased what in the 1860s was the largest ship in the world, a debt-inducing white elephant called the *Great Eastern*, which had been designed and built by the famous engineer Isambard Kingdom Brunel.

The *Great Eastern* was seven hundred feet long, drew fifty feet of water and had the capacity to carry four thousand passengers. It was built at Millwood, London, to transport immigrants to Australia and British troops to India. There hung on the wall of our living room a sketch of the *Great Eastern* that, in dim light, looked like a city skyline, all masts and sails and a calliope of smokestacks, a massive paddlewheel at the stern.

The *Great Eastern* was dogged by misfortune from the very start. The first attempt to launch it failed and resulted in great damage to the ship. Once launched, it brought grief to everyone involved with it.

Its bad luck was said to have been caused by a jinx placed on it during its construction when a rumour spread that two men were trapped somewhere between the hulls. Isambard Kingdom Brunel refused to tear apart his ship merely on the basis of a rumour, and so the hulls were sealed.

The rumours of faint tappings heard from within persisted throughout the life of the ship. These rumours scared off passengers afraid of hearing ghosts or afraid of being on board when God got round to exacting his revenge, or afraid of the bad luck that was said to hang for life on anyone who had anything to do with Brunel's floating masterpiece. Mystics predicted its every voyage would be its last. The sinking of the *Great Eastern* was foreseen a thousand times but never happened.

A failure as a passenger ship, its one great success was the laying of the transatlantic cable. It carried the three thousand miles of cable in its hold, played it out foot by foot until the last of it was sunk in a protective trench on the floor of the harbour at Heart's Content.

In 1887 the *Great Eastern* was sold for scrap. It took two years to dismantle it; in 1889 the skeletons not of two men, but of a man and a boy, a father and his twelve-year-old son, were found sealed between the hulls.

"Is that true?" I said.

"No," my father said. "No. It's just a story." But I knew from how he spoke that it was true.

He told me to imagine the *Great Eastern* as it hove to in sight of Newfoundland, still bound to Ireland by that cable that played out from the stern like some fishing line, as if it had trolled the Atlantic without success for some creature of the deep.

"They could have reeled the *Great Eastern* in from Ireland," my father said. "Or once the cable was ashore, we could have reeled in Ireland from Newfoundland."

Newfoundland and Ireland physically linked, tethered, bound together by a cable that, to this day, lies buried on the ocean floor. Was this not something marvellous? he said. But I would not be put off.

For how long had the man and his son remained alive? I asked. My father said they had survived for years by eating rats that like them had been trapped between the hulls and by licking condensation from the walls. I knew he was hoping that by making this joke, he would fool me into thinking the whole thing had been made up. I kept asking questions.

Why was their entrapment, their entombment, just a rumour and not a fact? Why was their disappearance not evidence enough of where they were?

"It's just a story," my father said.

What would they have talked about once they gave up hope of being rescued? Were they found side by side or far apart? Had they been able to hear sounds from outside? Probably, since people outside had been able to hear *them* tapping on the hull. Muffled sounds. A world away. Did they die while the ship was still being built, before it was even launched, or after it was launched?

"That's enough questions, Wayne," my father said. "You asked me for a story, so I made one up."

I put the questions to myself instead. What must it have been like in there, between the hulls? There would have been no light, or almost none. Dark, silent, with only each other to talk to and only each other to hear. It seemed at once terrifying and absurd, the two of them trapped between the hulls of that great ship while work on the exterior continued or while the *Great Eastern* was under sail.

The *Great Eastern* and its hull-haunting ghosts, the bones of a man and his son still clothed, their boots still on their bony feet. A father and his son. What a strange companionship their last days must have been. Companionship. Ship companions.

I lay awake for a long time, watching my father as he looked out the window and filled and refilled his glass with rye and ginger ale. The train rumbled along, swaying on the narrow gauge. We were passing through the core. Through the window, even though our car was dark, I could see only what the locomotive light eight cars ahead revealed, a short stretch of tracks, the reflection of the light as we crossed a stretch of open water. In the observation car it had been chilly, but underneath the blankets it was warm.

I fell asleep and sometime later was wakened by his voice. I was about to admit to him that I had been asleep when I realized he was not talking to me.

He spoke, inaudibly, paused as if to let someone reply, then spoke again. His voice was low. Some of what he said I could not make out. He drank, his head tipped back, eyes closed as though he was engrossed in this attempt to drain his glass. He poured another drink.

"Dad?" I said.

Startled, he froze in the act of raising his glass to his mouth. He lowered his arm.

"Thought you were asleep," he said.

"Who were you talking to?" I said.

"No one," he said. "There's no one here but you and me."

"What happened on the beach?" I said.

"What do you mean? Whatever I said, I said it in my sleep."

"You weren't asleep," I said, but he said nothing.

"I heard you and Harold once. At the Come Home Year party."

"I don't know what you think you heard. Just two men who had too much to drink, that's all. Go back to sleep now. No more questions."

I nodded off to the sound of him gulping from the glass. When I woke up in the morning he was still there in the chair, eyes closed, his head to one side and thrown back against the cushion, the glass, and the whisky and the ginger-ale bottles all scattered on the floor about his chair, all empty. He stayed that way until I woke him when we pulled into the station at St. John's.

One night, a few weeks later, presumably to wrench myself from a dream, though I remembered none of it, I threw myself right out of bed, out of the top bunk, and in the darkness struck my head on the bedpost of the other top bunk, cutting myself above the eye. I let out such a shriek that my parents heard me. They came running and, turning on the light, found me lying on the floor, blood streaming down one side of my face, my three terrified brothers sitting up with their backs against the wall as if I had attacked them in their sleep.

MARCH 12, 1947

They cut ice on Sundays for themselves and for the few people in town who can afford to hire help. There are some fridges in Ferryland, but most people, even most of those with money, still use what his father calls "real ice." His father speaks with scorn of the fridges he has seen, with their little freezers that can barely hold ten pounds of food.

They go far in behind the Gaze to where they know for certain that the ice is good, above the highest point of the old branch line and the runoff from the houses. They are known to cut a good crop of ice. His father estimates that the first fifty feet of the pond is frozen to the bottom. He says he bets there are trout trapped in the ice.

He laughs. Although this is a possibility his father firmly believes in, no one he knows has ever found a trout on the floor of their ice house in the fall.

This ice is opaque with frost, which has made its way from top to bottom through the airholes. This is the best sort of ice, compacted, compressed, dense white ice that even if it were not packed in sawdust would take months to melt. Ice drawn dripping from the water does not last half as long.

With axes, they chop through the rim ice that overlaps the shore until the exposed wedge is two feet thick. Then they switch to the two-handled ice saw that his father made in the forge.

He saws on his knees, from the shore, his father on the ice, half-kneeling, half-lying down, his hobnailed boots dug in. The saw is at an oblique angle, and ice dust flies up between them. It is awkward work but safer than sawing ice that might give way. There is no sound like that of ice being sawn, a rasping screech even higher pitched than the sound a hacksaw makes in metal.

They saw two parallel lines four feet apart, then use their augers to hack the block free. They push the jagged block of ice up the rim, then saw it even on both ends. They work for hours, moving out from shore until water bubbles up around the blade.

On its underside, the ice is encrusted with gravel and weeds where the floor of the pond has adhered to it. With the scrapers that they use to keep the runners free of snow, they scour the blocks like pelts until they gleam.

They work until it's getting dark, cutting more ice than the horses can pull, so they cover with boughs what they cannot take and will come back for it tomorrow. They light the lanterns and hang them on the rear uprights. He loves the journey back, ice piled block on block beneath a tarp and lashed onto the sled with ropes and chains. There is snow on the ground but none on the trees because it rained two days ago. He looks at the sky that, at twilight, changes colour every minute, looks at the bare black spruce along the shore, the two horses, the alternate bobbing of their heads and their behinds.

On the flats the horses pull the heavy sled with ease. When they reach the upward slope, he and his father walk beside the sled, push it where the slope is icy or the snow gives way. On the downgrades, they stand on the back runners, leaning into the turns to keep from swerving. At an especially steep downgrade they jump off and, each still holding an upright, are dragged along as though on skis, both leaning back, digging the heels of their boots in when they can to keep the sled from gathering so much momentum that it overtakes the horses.

They approach a stretch where the ground falls off sharply on the right. He and his father lean to their extreme left. Connie, because she is stronger, is on the sloped side of the path. Just for a moment, her right hoofs lose their purchase on the snow and the sled swerves wildly, almost in a semicircle. It has just begun to recoil, to right itself as they expect it to, when the traces snap loudly, both at once. His father shouts something.

As he tumbles, he hears the ice blocks clattering against each other. The sound is all around him, under him, above him, as if he is borne up by some of the blocks and some of them by him. Something he thinks might be the auger slams him in the back and he wonders if the saw will hit him next, if it is in there with him among the ice blocks, whirling lethally around. For the first time he hits the ground, hip and shoulder first, the best way to land, he just has time to think, before what must be alders lash his face. His knees come up hard against something, a rock he thinks, until he feels it give slightly, just enough to keep his legs from breaking. One of the ice blocks, it must be.

"*Art!*"

The shout comes from far above him, so far that he can barely hear it.

"*Down here,*" he says.

"*Are you all right?*"

He moves his legs, his arms, rises slowly to his feet.

"*I think so. Are you?*"

"*I'm all right. Is Gail down there? I got Connie.*"

He looks around but in the darkness can see nothing, not even the lanterns on the sled. "*Gail!*" he shouts over and over. In between, he listens for her. Surely, even if she were badly hurt, she would make some sound.

"*She must be up there somewhere.*"

"*All right. Come up.*"

He feels foolish. Here he is, gone flailing down a hill with a day's worth of ice while his father has not only not gone over with him but has somehow managed to keep hold of one of the horses.

Frantically he begins to climb the hill as if the sooner he meets his father at the top the less foolish he will seem to him. He feels what he would call a stitch or a cramp if it were in his side and not deep in his stomach. He climbs more slowly. The slope is steep, the snow a solid crust and for every three feet he climbs he slides back two. His father talks him up, saying "Here" every few seconds as if otherwise he would lose his way.

"I know where you are," he says, and after that his father says nothing.

It takes him more than an hour to get to the top and frequently he stops to rest. He looks back. If Gail was down there, he would hear her. But even if she were, what could he do? It must have been a frozen bog that he brought up on. There was ice but also tufts of sod beneath his feet. What a sight if he could see it. The sled overturned, the blocks of ice spread out like silver coffins on the bog.

A match flares up when he is almost at the top. "Can't waste more than one," his father says.

He sees the state of things. His father is holding Connie by the bridle. A splintered wooden shaft hangs from her collar. Everything else, rope reins, traces, even her bridle bit, are gone. There is blood on her mouth from where the bit tore loose. He can tell by her ears and eyes that if her father lets her go she will bolt. They have only had her for a week, and she does not trust them not to lead her straight back into trouble. It took forever that morning just to hitch her to the sled.

"No sign of Gail?" he says.

His father shakes his head. "She must have gone over with you," he says.

"Maybe she ran off."

"She wouldn't run off."

"I should have looked around for her."

"You were right not to," his father says. "Too dark."

"We should wait. She might be down there. Knocked out or something."

"We can't afford to wait. She'll come up if she can and find her own way home."

They will have to walk. If they still had Gail she might let them ride her. But Connie has never been ridden and will certainly bolt if they try to ride her now. They can't take the chance, for they will not make it home without her. There is no path to speak of, and without the lanterns they cannot see the tracks they made that morning. She will have to lead them home, following what little of her scent is left after more than half a day.

"We'll have to walk all night," he says, hoping his father will contradict him. His father says nothing. "It's going to snow," he says. He has known it for some time. He had calculated that it would start shortly before they got home, had been looking forward to the last leg of the trip, the two of them with their haul of ice standing on the back of their horse-drawn sled as it coasted downhill through the snow, a pair of lanterns glowing on the uprights. It's not a storm that's coming, just a fall of snow, but more than enough to mask the scent.

"Take the other side," his father says. "We'll have to go nice and slow. She'll be skittish for a while."

All he can see are the shapes of treetops, which are a faint shade darker than the sky. He is grateful that, somehow, in his fall, his hat stayed on. Something he is afraid to taste in case it might be blood runs down his face. Not blood, he decides. Too cold for blood. Not salty. If there was a moon, if the sky were not so overcast, if not for that faint breeze rising from the east portending snow —

"Friggin' stupid," his father says. To be here like this, he means, in country they are unfamiliar with, not to have taken more food with them than they could eat for lunch, not to have brought two pairs of boots, not to have dressed more warmly, to be so sure of themselves that they set out knowing that a fall of snow was on its way.

They have been walking for an hour and Connie is still fretful, still suspicious of them. His father walks with both hands on her bridle, but he can only manage one.

He stoops and picks up some snow.

"Don't eat that," his father says. He knows you're not supposed to, not even if you hold it in your mouth and let it melt before you swallow it, not even if you hold it there so long that it gets warm. "The heat that makes it warm comes from you," his father told him once. "Remember that. Lost heat that you might need." He knows this. He throws the snow aside. It takes longer to die of thirst than it takes to freeze to death. A lot longer. How many times has he heard that? And yet, if not for his father, he would have eaten it.

"We'll build a fire if we have to," his father says. If we can't go on, he means — if we have no choice but to try to keep it lit at night while snow that might as well be rain comes down. There is no way they will stop to start a fire.

After a while his arm is so tired that he cannot hold the bridle. He tells his father.

"We'll switch sides," his father says. "I'll switch first. Don't let go. Hold on with both hands until I tell you." His father ducks under Connie's neck. "Okay," he says.

He lets go of the bridle and falls to his knees. "I'm not that tired," he says, laughing, genuinely surprised, as if something other than exhaustion pulled him down. Connie tosses her head. His father says something soothing, rubs her neck with the palm of his hand. She knows now that they are relying on her. He has given it away. Or perhaps she has known it since the sled went down the slope, or since they set out without Gail.

"Can you get up?" his father asks. He is so sure he can he doesn't answer. But when he tries to, he winds up on all fours. Can it be that Connie is all that has been keeping him from falling? He tries again, rises slowly to his feet and feels his father's hand grip his upper arm, pull him and turn him about. He takes the bridle, swears to himself he will not make things harder for Connie by hanging from it as he knows he must have been doing before he fell. Only a few hours have passed since they lost the sled. He should not be this tired.

"I can't see anything," he says.

"Even so, don't close your eyes," his father says.

If he had the matches he would light one just to see something, some thing, some mundane thing, a bush, a rock, a clump of snow, a tree, some assurance that the world is as it always was and the night will pass.

What if Connie has lost the way and, like them, is simply walking? Perhaps she thinks they are leading her.

He knows the way home is not a straight line, but it seems to him that they are walking one. The boughs of spruce trees brush across his face, stinging his eyes. If he could, he would hold his free arm up to shield himself. The path, when they were coming in, was never so narrow that you had to duck beneath the branches. He wonders if they have strayed from it, kept going straight when they should have turned or turned when they should not have.

He cannot stop thinking that if it snows, Connie will lose the scent. That is all she has to guide her, and there is no scent less reliable than one left on snow, for snow is always changing. Even if the wind came up, loose snow sheltered from the rain by trees might drift across the path. A few times he has heard it, a sifting sound along the forest floor.

He tells himself he must not panic, that even if he only feels panic Connie will sense it and it will throw her off or she will bolt. Their task is simple. They must walk and go on walking, step after trusting step until she leads them home. There is nothing to wait for, nothing to decide. There is no suspense except about how fast the wind will rise and when the snow will start. She will do her part, so their survival is contingent on nothing but themselves.

As if he has said so out loud his father tells him, "Say your prayers. Just to keep your mind from wandering, I mean."

He nearly laughs, not at the notion of praying but at his father, not wanting him to panic, not wanting him to think that things are hopeless, yet telling him to pray.

He knows he ought to worry more about his father than himself. His father is in his mid-fifties. And yet he is breathing evenly and the few times that he speaks his voice is strong.

Because his father will not leave him, both of their lives depend on him, the weaker of the two. This is always how it is. He has heard stories of two men dying because one was hurt and the other would not leave him or did so too late to save himself. They live in a place where a man could die if he spends the night outdoors. He has always known this, but it has never struck him as ridiculous before.

He feels dizzy, thinks the world, if he could see it, would be spinning. The dizziness gives way to a kind of fatigue he has never known. He is surprised that this deep weariness has come on so suddenly. He always thought that if he were caught outdoors, he would get unbearably cold before he felt this way. But his body has gone straight to this beguiling enervation that tells him he must rest, that no harm and only good will come of it.

He misses now the energy he used to keep pace with his father when they sawed the blocks of ice. He wishes he had climbed that slope more slowly. "I think I hurt myself," he says, folding his free arm across his stomach. "When I fell, I must have hurt myself."

"I know," his father says. "Don't worry. It can't be all that bad."

He has known it all along. He lit the match so he could look him over and saw something in his face he didn't like. He has said nothing for fear of alarming him and making matters worse.

He doesn't know how long it's been since they switched sides on the bridle when the pain in his right arm gets so bad he has to let the bridle go. He falls to his knees again and Connie's flank butts him lightly as he hits the ground. She rears up, performs a clopping highstep, but no sound comes from her throat. Perhaps she is past the point of bolting now. Perhaps she feels like him. He leans his head against her flank to rest, to warm himself, but a cold lather is encrusted there and as he pulls away she rears up on her hind legs.

"I can't let go of her," his father says, and now his voice is not so strong. "Maybe I could use my belt and tie her to a tree."

Does he mean that if he lets go he too will fall? No. He means he cannot help him up. The wind is rising, still not blowing hard, but he can hear it in the trees. It does not sound too bad but it smells as if the snow is not far off.

It occurs to him that if he does not stand this time he never will, not even with his father's help. His arm is still upraised. He tried when he fell to let it drop, but when it came even with his shoulder something locked. He feels about for the bridle, puts his hand on Connie's face and slides it down until his fingers close about the leather strap. Then he grabs the bridle with his other hand and with a wrench that leaves him breathless makes it to his feet.

He is dying, but not from exposure. Somewhere inside he must be bleeding. That is why he is so thirsty. But how can he be dying if there is no pain, just this stitch that feels the same as it did when he first noticed it. He wonders if his father is so intent on keeping the horse calm that he cannot talk to him. He wants to talk. He wants to know how badly hurt his father thinks he is.

"How far?" he says.

"Not sure. Not too far."

"Too bad about Gail."

"Yes. She might turn up."

"All that ice."

"I put too much on the sled."

"No — I just meant all that work for nothing."

"Plenty more where that came from."

"I must have hurt myself."

"Try not to think about it. We'll make it home all right."

Word will have spread that they have not come home. He remembers his mother putting a lantern in the back window of their house one night when she heard that three men who had gone out to cut some wood had not come home. All the windows that back onto the Gaze will be lit up by now.

There is a sudden surge in the wind and he realizes that for some time he has been walking with his eyes closed. He opens them and sees what he takes to be the light of the lighthouse on the Head. It is dulled and faintly flickering as if down there it may already have begun to snow. But it can't have or the foghorn would be sounding. He puts his hands to his eyes and finds that they are blurred with tears, wind-bidden they must be, for he feels nothing.

"The lighthouse," he says, pointing.

His father grabs his hand. "No," he says. "I just lit a match — that's all."

He could not have lit a match in all this wind.

"Don't give up," his father says, which frightens him. "It can't be that much farther now."

Something so inimical, so contrary that it must be coming from outside him is inclining him away from what, deep in his soul, he knows is true. He wonders what this something will make him do, about what it will change his mind.

He is dying. Everything confirms it. He seems to be remembering the present, to be looking back at now from sometime in the future, some remove that fills him with nostalgia for things still close at hand.

He thinks of the referendum. He should think of more important things, of what he can say to his father to fool him into thinking that if he goes on ahead without him he can bring back help and save them both.

There is going to be a referendum, but no one knows exactly when. He would like to know what their margin of victory will be. "Think of the referendum not as a threat but as a chance for Newfoundlanders to renew their vows," the Major said. He will not be there when they renew their vows. He should renew his now, but he doesn't know the words. He heard the Major say it once. The vow. The pledge. The Major made it up. He has heard his father say it. He should ask him to recite it. What should he say to his father?

Twenty-one and he has been nowhere in the world but Newfoundland. He should stop thinking of it as an island, as a place set apart from others by the sea. An island, until you leave it, *is* the world.

He comes to with his forehead in the snow, his hands on either side. He is not prone but on all fours, his head hung down.

"Can you get up, Art?" his father says. Arthur. His father chose that name. His mother, just to tease him, calls him Reginald. His second name. Freda told him it was purely by accident that his parents named him after King Arthur. They did not know that Reginald meant "king."

"Can you get up, Art?"

Yes. He is not sure if he says the word out loud.

"If he won't get up, I'll have to carry him," his father says. "I don't think I can. I'm not sure what to do."

He sounds as though he's talking to himself or to the horse.

"She might not bolt. You never know. But she'll never let me put him on her back."

Sometimes on hot days when he was five or six, he went to the cellar and with his hands scraped the sawdust from the blocks of ice that had been there since his father and his uncle cut them in late winter from a pond above the Gaze. He put his face against the ice, his cheeks, his forehead, rubbed them against it until the ache became unbearable. Then he left the cellar and, facing into the wind, let the warm air dry the water from his skin, from his forehead which, for hours afterwards, felt as if someone's hand were pressed against it.

His father will not leave him, not even if he dies. He will tell himself his son is only resting and sit beside him in the snow. And so he can only save his father if he saves himself.

He feels himself rising.

He must be lifting me, he thinks. But when he opens his eyes his father is still there beside the horse.

As he reaches up to take her bridle Connie lowers her head.

I'm all right.

He thinks he says the words out loud but his father shows no sign.

Perhaps he is not really on his feet. He wonders if it might be some illusion that means the end is near. This is his last thought before he hears his father shout. How much time passes in between he does not know.

"*The end of the path.*"

It sounds as though his father has gone on ahead.

"*The end of the path.*"

Even when they're coming back, they call it that. The end of the path. It's where the path peters out as you go inland from the Gaze.

But when you're heading homeward, this is where the path begins.

MY FATHER WENT to agricultural college in Truro, Nova Scotia, in the fall of 1948. His intention was not to become a farmer but to work at the government-run Experimental Farm near St. John's as a technologist.

He did, for a time after graduation, work at the farm. It was the only job he ever liked, the only one he had a more than merely retrospective fondness for.

The Experimental Farm existed to answer one question: could crops and livestock be farmed in Newfoundland that would rival, in quality and cost, those grown elsewhere?

My father and the other technologists on the farm were told to "think of things not as useless but as yet unutilized." They were asked to enumerate the as-yet-unutilized agricultural resources of Newfoundland.

Much time and money was spent investigating the uses to which our as-yet-unutilized thirty thousand square miles of bogs and barrens could be put. My father studied ways of converting barrens into pasture land, of growing fodder and hay on peat bogs. He helped raise specimens of vegetables that were just as good as any farmed on the mainland and only several dozen times more expensive to produce.

The mainlander who had been brought in to run the farm believed that the "attitude" of Newfoundlanders had as much to do with the island's economic problems as, for instance, the short length of the Newfoundland growing season. He asked my father and the others to see as their mandate the completion of this sentence: "Because of its climate and geography, Newfoundland is ideally suited for the production of..."

For the technologists, finishing that sentence became a way to pass the time while working. Bent over their microscopes, they would each blurt out their contributions.

Because of its climate and geography, Newfoundland is ideally suited for the production of alcoholics, royal commissions, snow, unsolvable enigmas, self-pity, mosquitoes and black flies, inferiority complexes, delusions of grandeur, savage irony, impotent malice, unwarranted optimism, entirely justified despair, tall tales, pipe dreams, cannon fodder, children who bear an unnatural resemblance to their grandparents, expatriates.

In spite of the Experimental Farm, Newfoundland's only agricultural export in the fifties was blueberries, which grew best on once-valuable timberlands that had been accidentally destroyed by forest fires.

The federal government soon saw that Newfoundland's agricultural potential did not warrant a workforce the size of the one at the Experimental Farm, and my father and most of the others were let go.

Or rather, he was transferred, as he put it, "From land to sea." He wound up having no choice but to apply his lab technology skills to the fishery when, far from starting new ones, Newfoundlanders began to abandon what few farms there were.

His being hired by the Department of Fisheries was doubly ironic, first because his whole intention in attending agricultural college had been to eschew all connection with the fishery, and second because the job he had no choice but to accept was with the *federal* fisheries, which had begun operations in Newfoundland after the country's Confederation with Canada, the Confederation that he, his family and virtually all of Ferryland had bitterly opposed.

He lived in denial of these contradictions. By my time, he was well used to it. He had become what my mother called a "fishionary," part missionary, part visionary when it came to fish. Though he still regarded the sea with a mixture of awe, dread and revulsion, he preached the gospel of the fishery, predicted the imminent invention, by scientists and technologists like him, of new and more efficient ways of catching and preserving fish. Where the farm had failed, "the Station" would succeed.

The Station's official name was the Fisheries Research Board of Canada Biological Station. This was a grand name for a three-storey brick building on Water Street East that, though only completed in 1940, looked by the mid 1960s as if it was a hundred years old. The place was simply referred to as the Station. My father talked not about going to work but about going to the Station. "I have to be at the Station in twenty minutes," he'd say, saying "Station" as if he loved the place and could not wait to get there. Which may even have been true for a while.

My father became a fish man, a fish-preoccupied, fish-infatuated man, which, even in the island coastal city of St. John's was an oddball thing to be. The Station was regarded with scornful amusement by the people of St. John's, who, while they had no idea what went on inside it, were sure it was a variety of high-flown nonsense never heard of in Newfoundland before Confederation. Its long, ponderous name alone was proof of that.

But then there was the place itself. Its rooms were still lit late at night, and at the windows you could catch from the street as you were going by a glimpse of men in white lab coats and of strange-looking glass receptacles, and convoluted tubes and other apparatus. The Station was seven windows wide, and my father worked in the lab whose two windows were on the far left side of the second storey as you faced the building from Water Street. Before going into the Station, I imagined him in there, inscrutably engaged in the study of fish. It was more interesting to look at from the outside than to visit. The lab itself reeked of the gas that fuelled the Bunsen burners and of the algae-covered Petri dishes in which bacterial cultures and parasites were grown and scrutinized through microscopes. An air of profound boredom hung over the place and over the men who worked there and repeatedly conducted the same tests that gave the same results.

Still, my father steeped himself in fish lore. Even in the sixties he believed the Station would help keep alive the one industry that Newfoundland could count on, that would still be there when all of Joey's mills and mines and factories had been shut down. My father said that because of Joey Smallwood, the fishery was underused, swore that a thousand times as many cod as were being caught and sold were dying of old age.

My father would take me down onto the apron of the waterfront, which he said used to be lined with cargo ships into which blocks of saltfish were loaded like cords of wood. Now fish no longer had to be salted. Now freezer trawlers docked at harbour side. Their great, cavern-like freezers, when opened to the air, emitted blasts of steam, as if their insides were on fire.

My father taught me about fish — not about how to catch them, but about the fish themselves, how to tell one kind from another, not just when they were still whole but when they were fillets in the supermarket. He taught me how you could tell from looking at fish if it had been frozen or when it was caught. He taught me where in the ocean each type of fish came from and at what depths they could be found, how what they ate affected how they tasted, how to tell from how they tasted what they ate, how to tell how old they were by examining their skeletons — toting up the cartilaginous layers was much like counting tree rings — how cold, how salty was the water they lived in, the various parasites that preyed on each fish, the microorganisms they were composed of, how each fish was best preserved and processed.

It was some sort of an escape from fishing itself, this knowledge that he shared with me and whose acquisition was not required by his job. Sometimes it seemed that he was contriving a fascination with the ocean that he did not feel, as if he was trying to fool it into thinking that it didn't really have him, or that it did but that he didn't mind, that even if he were free to choose he would live the way he did and his lack of choice was therefore irrelevant. But the chain was not severed; it was only longer than it would have been had he remained a fisherman, longer and easier to disguise as something else.

He tried to teach me the Latin names of fish.

Latin, Latin, Latin. It seemed that that was all I heard from him for years. The way he pronounced it, they way he playfully spoke it *at* me always got me laughing. Sometimes, talking to my mother, he parodied the suave, debonair, literally Latin lover, rhyming off in Latin the names of fish. Cod: *Gadus morrhua.*

"*Gadus morrhua?*" my father would say, proffering a forkful of cod at me. I thought he was making most of it up, though in fact he wasn't. He told me that the Latin name of the tomcod, a small, permanently immature species of cod, was *Microgadus tomcod.* Who could blame me for doubting that that was made up? Herring: *Clupea haerengus haerengus*; tuna: *Thunnus thynnus* — "Two tins of *Thunnus thynnus*, thank you," my father said in grocery stores; turbot: *Reinhardtius hippoglossides.* My favourite was halibut, *Hippoglossus hippoglossus.* I absolutely refused to believe that this was its name. Mackerel: *Scomber scombrus.* These, he told me, had no air bladder, what in the cod was called a "sound," and so had to swim continuously to keep from sinking. There was the northern shrimp, *Pandalus borealis*, not to be confused with striped shrimp, *Pandalus montagni.*

These were in fact their abbreviated names, their genus and species. A fish's full name, my father told me, consisted of — all in Latin — its genus, species, family, order, class, phylum and kingdom.

All through my childhood he told me about fish, more about them than I wanted to know. There were the various kinds of flatfish, for instance, the witch flounder and the winter flounder and the turbot.

The flatfish started out life with its eyes arranged like those of other fish, but in the first months of its life, one of its eyes slowly moved to the other side of its head so that both eyes were on the same side, necessitating that the fish swim with its eyeless blind side against the ocean floor, which it so perfectly resembled it was absolutely invisible until it moved. Otherwise it lay there, its tandem of same-side eyes barely open, keeping watch for prey and predators, a master of camouflage looking up from the ocean floor. My father had a "flatfish face" that he used to do for me and that always sent me into hysterics.

He told me that the largest codfish ever caught and recorded had weighed 211½ pounds, had a platter-size tongue that had weighed three pounds and had made a meal for six people. It was known among fishery biologists as "Gadus the Great." Some people at the Station referred to the codfish in general as "Gadus the Great."

He told me that cod was so plentiful on the Grand Banks because of the plankton conveyed south by the Labrador Current. Nowhere in the world was there a plankton feeding ground compared with that of the Grand Banks, and it was all due to the Labrador Current. When I first heard of the Labrador Current, I could not help imagining a river that originated in the heart of the Labrador wilderness and by which plankton was borne along to the North Atlantic.

And then there were the capelin. There was no fish easier to catch than capelin, for they literally rolled up in waves on the beaches.

"The capelin are in," my father said excitedly, waking me up one Sunday morning in June after having just got the word from Gordon in Ferryland. They were not in at Bay Bulls or Witless Bay but they were in at Ferryland. The whole family, not bothering with breakfast, piled into the car.

The winter had been cold, spring had come late, but at last the capelin had come ashore to spawn, and with the spawning capelin came the cod; on the beach below the Gaze a mass mating was taking place, the females leaving their eggs buried in the sand where they were insulated from the icy water; once the eggs hatched, they would be carried out to sea with each retreating tide.

The capelin, as if in mass surrender to our species, rolled up on the shore in waves, black waves alive with little fish that, once marooned, flopped about in millions on the sand, olive green on top, silver on the bottom. From a distance, from the height of the house above the sea, it appeared that the water of the coastline had turned black.

By the time we got down to the beach, there were half a dozen stocky, shaggy-maned ponies lined up on the sand at an angle to the water, waiting patiently to serve their purpose, harnessed to carts that had large-spoked wooden wheels. Fishermen wearing rubber kneeboots and tweed sod caps used long-handled dip nets to scoop the capelin from the water and dump them in the carts.

It could have been a scene from a hundred years ago, from June of 1869. The beach swarmed not only with capelin but with children, running about up to their knees in the little fish, each wave being about two parts capelin and one part water. We took off our boots and socks and waded into the capelin. I felt the shock of the icy water on my shins. My feet went numb. I reached down and grabbed two fistfuls of fish, writhing, struggling half-foot-long fish. When I held them to the sun a certain way, I saw, among the olive and silver, iridescent pinks and greens and blues. What a strange bounty it was. I looked about. Dead capelin littered the beach, decaying, drying in the sun, trodden into the wet sand by the horses whose hooves left little craters that filled up with water.

"*Mallotus villosus* Muller!" my father shouted, chasing my mother down the beach, in one hand a capelin that he said he was going to shove down her dress.

We followed the horses and their carts with their teeming mounds of fish flesh as they plodded down the beach towards the road to the wharf. As they struggled up over the steep incline between beach and road, hoofs slipping, we and several dozen children of Ferryland helped them, pushed the carts, the wooden wheels, cheered when they crested the hill.

We filed along the roadside, a procession of ponies pulling carts of capelin, and fifty or sixty children with dogs trotting along beside us, trying to assert their importance by barking at the ponies who ignored them.

When I looked back I saw my parents.

My father was sitting on the beach rocks, knees drawn up, arms resting on them, head hung down in a posture of dejection. My mother stood beside him, one hand on his shoulder, looking out to sea between the islands. She bent over and said something. Gently he dismissed her with a wave of his hand, gestured at us as if to remind her we were watching. She seemed to shrug and began walking down the beach towards us.

ONE OF HIS duties at the lab was to grade fish from plants around the island A, B, or C, and this involved tasting endless samples of boiled fish, usually cod.

This is how he was engaged when our school had "What Does Your Father Do?" Day when I was twelve, and each of us spent a day on the job with our fathers.

My father and several others sat at a table for the whole day tasting fish, using spit buckets the way television actors making food commercials do. Between tastes, they gargled palate-cleansing water, which they likewise spat into the buckets. A woman circulated constantly, refilling their glasses, a jug of water in each hand. In a little kitchen just off the lab, a small assembly line of men and women wearing plastic caps bent over boilers, prepared the fish, took paper plates from the stacks inside the door and put on each plate one square inch of fish, which were then conveyed to the tasters by a procession of servers.

When the plates were put in front of them, the tasters first rubbed a morsel of the cod between their thumbs and index fingers. Then they smelled it, bending their heads to the plates.

Finally they tasted it and silently recorded their grades on a kind of scorecard. These were to be averaged to determine the grade of the fish. That was how it was supposed to work.

A big, bald, red-faced man whose lab coat could barely contain his bulging arms kept spoiling the taste tests by protesting out loud each time what he deemed to be a bad batch of fish came his way. "Jesus, honourable *God*," he said, spewing fish into his bucket.

This upset everyone because it meant that this batch of fish would have to be tested again, that it would go back with the as-yet-untasted batches and at some random point be put in front of them. My father said they should put the red-faced man at the end of the line and then his reactions would not affect the grades the others gave the fish, but the man running the tests said it didn't matter what order they used, for any outward displays of like or dislike might confuse their judgment of the fish that followed.

"I don't like fish no matter what grade it is," the red-faced man said. "I just don't like fish. I shouldn't have to taste it if I don't like it."

"Everyone has to take their turn," the manager said, explaining that if he did not take his, the others would be assigned an extra day of fish tasting every couple of months.

"Is this how any man should have to spend his days?" the red-faced man said, turning his rheumy gaze on me. "Two days every month," he said, as if on the verge of tears, "two days every month."

My father would come home from days spent in this manner not actually having eaten anything but unable to stand the sight or smell of food, his tastebuds so infused with fish that even the crackers he did eat hours later before bedtime still tasted of it.

But he was not turned from fish by the taste tests. He made fish-head stew, boiling the fish heads with potatoes and onions, and ate every part except the eyes, which I dared him to eat just to see how revolting it would look. There would be nothing left on his plate but pieces of quill-like cartilage and assorted cod skulls picked clean. If he wasn't going to eat the eyes, I asked him, why didn't he remove them before he put the fish heads on to boil, but he said it was simply too much of a bother. I can still see them, the inedible eyeballs of the cod, eyeballs the size of large marbles bulging goiterishly from the otherwise bare skulls. As my father wrestled with the heads, which were about as easy to pick meat from as Cornish hens, the eyes would roll around every which way, nothing but the whites showing sometimes.

In the summer, pairs of boys would walk up from Petty Harbour on weekend afternoons, each pair lugging between them a pail of cod tongues that had been cut from fish their fathers caught that morning. They went from door to door, offering the cod tongues for sale by the dozen.

As soon as those boys appeared, straining to keep their brim-full red or blue or yellow plastic buckets clear of the ground, the tongues slopping about like water, word spread through the neighbourhood.

The boys did not wait for people to come out to the ends of their driveways, for they were in haste to sell their tongues before they went off, as they quickly did in the heat of summer.

The tongues — they were not really "tongues," but just the fleshy parts on the floor of the cod's mouth — were pink

on the bottom and had a semi-translucent white skin on the top.
Cooked properly, pan-fried with flour and butter or little cubes
of fat-back called scruncheons, they were one part jelly, three
parts meat and delicious beyond imagining, as far as I was concerned, though not everyone agreed with me.

I looked forward to the first cod tongues of the year
almost as much as I looked forward to Christmas or Halloween.
My father got a kick out of my fondness for a delicacy that most
children, including all my brothers and sisters, turned up their
noses at, and though he was probably not as mad about them
as I was, it became an event for him and me to share what he
called "a feed of tongues." We went to the front door together when the boys from Petty Harbour laboured up the steps.

"How much are they?" my father would say, though he
knew they always sold for about a dime a dozen. He would buy
seven or eight dozen, give the boys a dollar bill and let them
keep the change. They dipped their hands into the mass of slick,
round tongues, not counting them out but estimating by weight
the number of dozen he asked for, slopping them into the plastic bags or the sheets of waxed paper we provided for them,
for they carried no such supplies of their own, just the tongues
in the uncovered buckets. While one of them doled out the
tongues, the other kept an anxious eye on the other pairs of
boys to see how far ahead of them they were.

I envied them, the boys of Petty Harbour in their grimy
coveralls and fish-blood-smeared T-shirts and rubber boots,
watched them as they sold their unsanctioned, uninspected cod
tongues to my father, an officer with the federal Fisheries
Department. They were selling the tongues for their fathers
and probably did not have a cent to call their own, but I either

didn't know this or didn't stop long enough to consider the terms of their existence. When they came up the road, two to a bucket, I regarded them as if they were selling the surplus of some feast they had had or would soon have, these boys who had so many more cod tongues than they could eat that they sold them from door to door.

The tongues were a gelatinous, undifferentiated mass inside the plastic bags. I would squeeze them lightly in my hands, revelling in their texture and their faintly fishy smell. My father would place the bag in a bowl of cold water, which he would leave on the counter until suppertime, for cod tongues suffered from even a few hours in the fridge.

My father cooked the tongues while I sat waiting at the kitchen table, the house empty except for us, the others having fled to escape the smell of fish frying. As we ate, washing down the tongues with mugs of tea, I told my father that next time we should buy a whole bucketful, just to see how many we could eat at one sitting. I could not imagine there being any limit.

We often went down to Petty Harbour and bought a whole codfish from one of the fishermen who sold them straight off the wharf. My father always took great pride in answering no when the fishermen asked him if he would like to have his fish cleaned and filleted. He would always do something to impress the fishermen, demonstrate some skill or knowledge that even they did not have. By lifting it by the gills with one hand, he could estimate a cod's weight within a few ounces. He was usually so close to the weight that showed on their scales that the fishermen shook their heads in disbelief. Then he would overdo it, and tell them how old the fish was, and how you could tell how old it was, and in what depth and temperature of water it had lived and been caught. "You know your fish, sir," they'd say more politely than admiringly, for this was not fishermen's knowledge that he was displaying, not knowledge that would be of any real use to fishermen. He had been one of them once, and a part of him really did want to impress them and win their admiration and acceptance.

They were painfully awkward, those trips to Petty Harbour, where he tried to be both things at once and could not completely pledge himself to either, the lab man of the "New Newfoundland" and the fisherman he used to be. The drive back home was always made in silence.

SOME SATURDAYS, WHEN my father had to work overtime, we drove to town with him and, while he was at the Station, went shopping or to visit his sister Eva and her husband, Jim, who ran a little confectionery near the Capital theatre on Henry Street.

The tarred, flat-topped roof of her house glistened in the rain. In Eva's house, when conversation lagged, we sat about in muted gloom, the only sound the city sound of tires on wet pavement on a weekend afternoon. I thought it must have been like this in every house in the old Catholic sections of the city. These were houses to which children, once they left, did not return for years, waiting until the hold the place had on them had weakened to the point that they were sure they could withstand it. There was a sense in these neighbourhoods not that time had stopped but that its passage was marked by events unheard of by outsiders.

The houses in Eva's neighbourhood had no front yards, none at all; nothing separated house from sidewalk. Ancient sheer curtains, a compromise between the need for light and the need for privacy, were drawn in most of the front windows within inches of where pedestrians passed. Leading up to the front door was a single or perhaps a pair of concrete slabs two feet high and wide and jutting out to claim a token portion of the sidewalk. People sat out on these glorified steps after supper, men in white undershirts and women in ragged dresses, drinking from stubby brown bottles marked Dominion Ale, named not for the Dominion of Canada but the short-lived Dominion of Newfoundland.

In these rough neighbourhoods for which the word "slums" was at once somehow too grand and too unfair a word, my parents had once lived, moving from one house to another, endlessly moving as it seemed all the Johnstons who had left Ferryland and the Everards who had left the Goulds were fated to do, trying to save enough to buy one of these houses that it seemed even the poorest of the poor could afford, yet somehow they could not.

It seemed to me that whenever the sun came out, it was always after days of rain, a reprieve. Suddenly the streets were teeming with children who, either happily ignorant of their deprivations or temporarily forgetting them, ran about in grime-ridden rags. The water on the pavement evaporated instantly, continent-like dry spots spreading out across the road.

Throughout this city, among all these hill houses on referendum night, July 22, 1948, shotguns had been fired in celebration, though it must have seemed to the losers that they were being symbolically executed, or as if the gleeful confederates were blowing their last faint hopes to smithereens.

In my parents' neighbourhoods, makeshift flags of mourning, most of them flour sacks dyed black with boot polish, hung above these houses on April 1, 1949, while the Pink, White and

Green, wherever it flew, did so at half-mast. It had been nine months since the referendum, nine months during which anti-confederates had felt as if they were waiting for a sentence of death to be carried out.

Aunt Eva seemed to me to be a city woman. Though they all lived in St. John's at one time or another, she was the only one of the Johnstons who stayed there for good. She seemed to know every square inch of St. John's. On these Saturdays, while my father worked late at the Station, we went out walking with her. I remember the blare of accordions from inside taverns whose open doors we sauntered past on summer afternoons, the view of the harbour from her office in the Sir Humphrey Gilbert Building, where the elevator stopped and started like a badly driven car, the big windows through which you could see all the ships moored bow to stern around the harbour, and on the South Side below the Brow the massive white oil tanks with the name IRVING written on them.

Eva told us stories about what St. John's was like before Confederation. There had been a bus system of sorts since 1939 run by the Golden Arrow Coaches Company of Nova Scotia. The buses were not well used because traffic in St. John's, in keeping with colonial practice, drove on the left, and the doors of these Canadian buses opened on the right, so that bus passengers were obliged to disembark straight into the stream of traffic.

Right-hand driving was unofficially adopted in St. John's in 1942. That its adoption was unofficial was unfortunate. Many Newfoundlanders drove on the left side of the road, others on the right, while also on the right drove baffled American and Canadian servicemen, and the British servicemen drove on the left. Troop trucks collided with motor cars; motorists of various nationalities, civilians and armed forces personnel swore at each other, got out of their cars and wound up in fistfights. Finally right-hand driving was officially adopted in 1947. By that time the Golden Arrow coaches were in such a state of disrepair after eight years of making their way back and forth the cobblestone length of Water Street that the whole fleet was in need of being replaced, which the company said it would agree to do only if Water Street was paved.

And so the paving of Water Street was the first great post-Confederation project. Eva said that people thronged the sides of the street to gawk and cheer as if the paving machines were floats in some parade, marvelling at the steaming asphalt, the motorized steamrollers. She shook her head as if the paving of Water Street was the beginning of the end of something.

After my father finished work at the Station and we had had dinner at Eva's, we went to the Capital movie theatre, the only place left in Newfoundland where people still protested en masse against Confederation. Long after the age of newsreels had passed, the proprietors of the Capital played Confederation-celebrating newsreels before the features, knowing that it was as much to boo and denounce the newsreels as to see the movies that audiences came out.

It was as ritualistic a prelude to the showing of a movie at the Capital as the playing and the singing of "The Ode to Newfoundland." There would be Joey, the star attraction at some federal Liberal convention in Ottawa, hobnobbing with Canadian politicians and bigwigs of all sorts. The audience laughed scornfully, swore, screamed, threw things.

But there were no riots, fistfights, no scuffles, because no one jumped to his feet to defend the absent Joey from his detractors or even sat in silent protest. One out of three in the city had voted for Confederation, but it seemed as if no one had, for you could not find one out of ten who would admit to it. Where *was* the confederate one-third, my father wanted to know. It seemed that everyone was a patriot now that to be one cost nothing, now that you could have your Canada and hate it too.

One newsreel, that of "the moment" itself, I saw only once. It reduced the audience, for a while at least, to a kind of mute brooding.

The "Ode to Newfoundland" was played and loudly sung. All the men, with their hats removed, belted out "The Ode"; all the women with their hats still on did likewise. Then, while they were still standing, while their patriotic fervour was still up, came the supposed newsreel salute to Joey and Confederation. For a while no one spoke. They watched as though amazed that "the moment" had been recorded, pre-served, that it was possible to do such things.

On the screen it is noon, April 1, 1949; in the Government House drawing room, beneath a massive sparkling chandelier, in front of a roaring fireplace, Albert Walsh is sworn in as Newfoundland's new lieutenant governor by the Canadian secretary of state, Colin Gibson. Walsh then swears in Joey as Newfoundland's first premier and swears in the members of the first provincial cabinet.

Alone of all the people on the screen, Joey seems to know where the camera is, its location and significance. Everyone else looks at the documents spread out on the table, the pen as it moves across the page, but Joey, knowing that history and the enemy are watching, looks at the camera. It is as if he can see all the people who in the future will be watching him, can foresee how it will gall the moviegoers of St. John's to have him beam at them in the instant before his swearing in, the *coup de grâce* for their country.

He seems to foresee, too, the cheering crowds of Canadian moviegoers, as well as the nostalgic Newfoundlanders in the moviehouses of Boston, New York, Baltimore and Philadelphia, the jeering expatriates who by moving away had lost their right to vote in the referendum and whose one hope of alleviating their homesickness and their guilt was that Newfoundland would join the States.

Finally the audience roused itself and began to boo and to throw things at the screen. Had they listened, they would have heard the narrator in a March-of-Time-like voice announce, "And so, with one stroke of the pen, Canada welcomes its tenth and newest province, Newfoundland, into Confederation, completing the Dominion of Canada from sea to sea. Not since 1871, when our most western province joined..."

But the audience booed loudly until the newsreel ended, shouted "Traitor!" and "Turncoat!" and "Backstabber!" while Joey smiled owlishly at them in black and white from the giant screen, his horn-rimmed spectacles gleaming.

The instant the newsreel ended, a calm fell on the moviegoers, who settled into their seats as perfunctorily as an about-to-be sermonized congregation. Then the movie, an American one, began, and there appeared on the screen a world in which Canada did not exist and in which the non-existence of Newfoundland the nation was somehow irrelevant, a world that despite Confederation was the same it had always been. In this movie world, there was no sudden severance from the past, the seventies were what in the forties people had expected they would be, history proceeding as advertised from one decade to the next. Joey, it must have been almost possible to pretend, was just a newsreel villain who could be mocked out of existence.

THEY ARE HEADING west, an hour out of Fortune with the engine at full throttle.

It is two years since he was made inspector. It was not a promotion but his children think it was. He travels the inaccessible-except-by-boat south coast with a group of other inspectors on a boat called the *Belle Bay*.

His family was with him the first time he saw the *Belle Bay*. It was docked in St. John's harbour. It was much smaller than he expected. He had formed an impression of it from stories he had heard of storms that it survived at sea.

As he drove along the apron of the waterfront to where the *Belle Bay* was docked, he passed a good many ships moored with hawser ropes as thick as schooner masts. He would not have been disappointed to be told that any one of them was the *Belle Bay*. But the *Belle Bay* was tucked in between two such ships, as if it had been expertly parallel parked, and he could barely see its radar pole above the dock. To board it you had to walk down a rickety gangplank. It was at least modern, almost new, in fact, with a rounded fibreglass hull. It had the moulded, watertight look of a capsule that would stay afloat while on its side or even upside down.

The boat was being readied for departure by a man who introduced himself as "the skipper," who seemed to think that by giving each of the children an apple he could hide from them the fact that he was drunk.

"It's pretty small," his wife said, staring at the boat.

"Oh, it's just a pup of a tub," the skipper said. It seemed he was about to add some reassuring qualification of this remark, but then he walked away.

He looks around, surveys what for weeks will be his home.

It has six sleeping bunks crammed into one end and an unbelievably compact laboratory at the other, trays of test tubes and beakers, and glass slides for storing microscopic samples and a battery of three microscopes mounted like miniature cannon along one wall.

There is a galley about a quarter the size of their kitchen at home. No one is allowed to set foot there but the cook, whose sole job it is to make meals for six men. There is a little wheelhouse above the foredeck for the skipper. The *Belle Bay* is white all over and flies two flags, the Canadian Maple Leaf and the Union Jack.

His fellows on the south-coast run are a man named Broadhurst, another named Manning, both about his age, a twenty-nine-year-old who looks like a teenager whom they call "Young Hunt," the skipper and the cook. On the morning of their first voyage, they seemed to him as unpromising a crew as he had ever seen. Nothing they have done since has made him change his mind.

Telling his sons anecdotes about his trips, he speaks these

names as soldiers do those of the men they went through combat with, the men of a platoon whose trials and afflictions were unprecedented and the full extent of which only they who have been through them can understand.

They set out every fortnight, congregating at dockside in the morning with their bags and their equipment, wearing black overcoats or parkas that identify them as federal Fisheries inspectors, blue-and-yellow badges on their shoulders. After the skipper, he is looked on as the seaman of the group. How far he is from being a seaman only the skipper knows. All the others are from St. John's and spent little or no time on the water before they were assigned to the *Belle Bay*.

Although he is spending more time on the water now than he did when he was young, his body has not changed. He still gets sick just once and only once each time they put out to sea.

The others seem to think he wills himself to be sick, as if this is a bit of sea savvy he picked up long ago: get sick as soon as you set sail and after that you'll be all right. He wouldn't be surprised to see Young Hunt try it — not that he would blame him, for Young Hunt is always sick. There have been times that such was his state that they all but wrote him off. He is a sickly looking fellow, even on dry land, pale, freckle-faced, very slightly built, with red hair as long as the department will allow, combed across his forehead so that when he stands with his head hung down, his hair obscures his face. Broadhurst is able to resist the urge to be sick in almost any weather, but once he starts he cannot stop. Manning is fine until he starts drinking, which he vows not to do, but he always gets so bored that after a few days, he cannot help himself.

He has begun keeping a log of his life, not just of his time on the water but his whole life. A "log" is a better word for this record than "diary" or "journal" because of the style in which he writes it. The entries that have to do with the south-coast trips read like those of the last-surviving member of some doomed expedition, the laconic voice of a man resigned to the fact that he is writing for posterity, that he must record the tale for he will never live to tell it. "May 19, 1971. Thirty miles from Gaultois. Can't keep anything down. Young Hunt always sick. Hasn't left his bunk since Tuesday. Broadhurst in better spirits today. Manning and the skipper drinking all day long."

There is a storm a hundred miles to the west, which, if they turn around, the skipper says, "might or might not" catch them before they make St. John's. Instead of deciding what to do, the skipper lets them put it to a vote. In the long run, turning back will just mean an extra three days away from home. They all vote to go on. He voted first, and the others followed his example while the skipper sat back watching and said nothing.

They are in rough water now. They are not in trouble, but Young Hunt has been asking him for hours what he thinks their chances are, if he has ever seen a sea as bad as this one. None of them ever consult the skipper on such things, as he never seems the least bit concerned no matter what their circumstances. On the rare occasion when one of them does ask him something, he tells them to "go play with their toys," by which he means their microscopes.

He knows that to Young Hunt he is living proof that they have nothing to fear from any sea that is not as bad as the worst one he has ever seen, so he is constantly asking him "Have you ever seen it this bad, Art?" This is just what he asked his father when he made his first trips in the punt when he was twelve. "Have you ever seen a storm like this?"

"Never," his father would say, winking at his older brother. "Worst I've ever seen."

He tells Young Hunt that the best thing he can do is go to bed and try to sleep.

The bunks are equipped with straps that when fastened keep him and the others from being tossed out of bed in rough weather. It is a strange thing to lie in bed in a storm-tossed boat. One second you are upside down, praying your restraints will hold, the next "standing" erect like a mummy, head up as the ship plunges into a trough and then feet up as the ship climbs to the crest of the next wave. Standing in the vertical ship, they turn their heads and look at one another, each gauging by the angle of the other person's body if the boat is going past vertical on its way to turning upside down.

"I can't stand it in the bunk," Young Hunt says. The only other thing to do is drink. Young Hunt digs his rum out from under his bunk and the others join him.

They leave it to him to decide when the skipper is "too far gone" to be trusted at the wheel.

The skipper, though he knows the south coast as well as anyone and is a master seaman, is so often drunk that "mutinies" are commonplace. Several times he and the others have strapped the skipper into his bunk, after which he has piloted the boat as best he can, the skipper roaring that he would have them arrested, that the RCMP would be waiting for them at dockside in St. John's. But there is a stalemate between skipper and crew; he dares not inform on them for fear it will come out that he operates the boat while drunk, and they dare not inform on him for fear they will be charged with mutiny.

By now, he is so concerned that he replies, "I don't know," when Young Hunt says, "Are we going to be lost, Mr. Johnston?"

Young Hunt is so fear-struck by this answer that he falls silent, staring out the window at the surging water as if it makes no sense that all this is being staged just for his extinction.

For a second, the *Belle Bay* lists almost to the point of turning over completely onto its starboard side. They pass within a few feet of a clanging bell that warns of submerged rocks.

"We're too close to the shore," he says and goes up top. He stands outside between the cabin and the rail and tries to gauge how much higher the swell is than it was at nine o'clock. He goes up to the wheelhouse. The skipper does not make even a token effort to hide the glass of rum beside the wheel.

He tries to convince the skipper to keep steering straight into the waves, but the skipper is inclined to "run," that is, travel with the waves, which increases the chances of being swamped from the stern since you cannot see what is coming at you. Running from a storm has its advantages, though, especially in the most extreme weather, when a ship's hull might not hold up against the sea, and the waves are so large and the crest of one so far from that of the next that it is possible, if you have all your wits about you, to sail along between the crests, keeping perfect pace with the storm. But these waves are not big enough for that, and the skipper is well on his way to being drunk. The hull hits a wave with a sound like the head-on collision of two cars, and the skipper yells, "It's time to run!"

"There's not enough room between the crests!" he shouts. "We'll be swamped!"

"Go play with your toys," the skipper says and begins the slow process of bringing the boat about.

He doubts that in his state the skipper will even manage that manoeuvre. He goes down below. Young Hunt is drinking rum straight from the bottle, hoping for an oblivion, a descent into sleep that in these circumstances no amount of booze will bring.

He looks at Broadhurst and Manning.

"Are you sure?" says Broadhurst.

He nods.

The trip has been routine for the first eight days. Rencontre East, Rencontre West, Boxey Harbour, McCallum, Mosquito, Goblin, Harbour Breton, Isles aux Morts, Gaultois. They have "hit" all these and are still on schedule. They have issued just three warnings. No catch of cod has been dumped, and no fish plant has been closed.

The south-coast settlements are by far the most isolated on the island. The cross-island highway is more than two hundred miles of uncharted wilderness away. One community is connected, if at all, to its neighbour on the coast by a footpath through the woods.

Though most of these remote outports voted overwhelmingly in favour of Confederation, they consider the inspectors to be their arch-enemies since they can, as it seems to the fishermen, order them on a whim to dump their entire catch, deeming it to have been improperly stored or preserved, or on a whim close down a fish plant because its standards are too low. To the fishermen, they are meddlesome townies, not men who make an honest living from the sea but men whose knowledge of the sea and fish comes from books and is therefore beneath contempt. In these tiny places, there is no one to enforce the law, no one they can appeal to for protection.

But all has gone well.

They walked about each settlement after work, had dinner at its one eatery, risked a drink at its one tavern, the six of them staying together, forever vigilant, sticking out like sore thumbs in their uniforms, which they thought it best to wear as reminders that anyone who trifled with them would have to answer for it.

There was not much to do. They grew bored, as always. They smoked, played cards, drank too much. They spoke to anyone who seemed not to know who they were or not to care. They left the taverns, stood side by side, the six of them, leaning on fences and breakwaters, looking out to sea as it was getting dark, the end of yet another day, putting off for as long as possible their return to the claustrophobic confines of the boat. They spent their nights in their bunks at dockside and moved on in the morning. All has gone well and now it is day nine of their inspection tour.

They round the point to head into a harbour. Word of their coming must somehow have spread, for they see hordes of people running about among the houses perched on the hills, people running to and from the fish plant, on the beach a line of fishermen making for the wharf. It is as if the whole town is putting into effect some long-established, much-rehearsed invasion-repulsion plan.

When they dock, all except the skipper and the cook disembark. They are met on the wharf by a man they take to

be the fish-plant manager. He wears a suit but no tie, a pale
yellow shirt with a white T-shirt underneath.

He assures them they are welcome but wonders if they
would like to have a drink before they go about their work.
Broadhurst politely declines the offer.

The man says that to spare them the trouble he will go
up to the plant and bring them back a sample of their fish.
Broadhurst shakes his head. "We have to inspect the plant,"
he says.

He leads an ever-growing delegation along the road that
leads up from the beach to the fish plant. Fishermen follow them.
Children come running from the school just up the hill. Women
walk beside them and in front of them, but no one says a word.

It is apparent the instant they set foot inside the plant that
they will have to close it down. The place reeks of fish gone or
going bad. Young Hunt stifles the urge to gag, takes his white
helmet off and puts it over his face so that only his eyes are
showing. The man who met them at the wharf gives him a look.

They go through the motions of inspecting the plant. They
have to. Something tells him it might be their only hope of
escaping unmolested. Young Hunt still holds his helmet to his
face. It looks like an oversize surgical mask.

The manager and sundry others who came up with them
from the beach follow them about and, despite Young Hunt,
look hopefully at them as if to say, You see, everything is in
good shape.

They walk about, tell fish cutters at whose elbows they
stand and over whose shoulders they look to pay no attention
to them, to go on about their work as usual. They jot things
down on their clipboards, fill out their report sheets.

The cutters wield foot-long knives. He watches one behead, debone and eviscerate a codfish faster than he has ever seen it done. He guesses it took twenty seconds.

The cutters stand in a line between a conveyor belt on which the codfish comes to them and a bench on which rest, one for each cutter, large plastic tubs that the cleaned fish are tossed into, while the head, guts and sound bones are thrown into other buckets on the floor. In addition, there are smaller buckets for the cod tongues and livers. These men wear plastic hats like shower caps, rubber gloves, rubber boots and once-white coats. Off to the other side of the plant, men and women package fish in small white cardboard boxes. It all looks just as it should.

"We'll have to take some samples," Broadhurst says. He picks up three packages of fish.

They take the samples down to the floating lab, once again escorted in silence by the locals, the plant workers included this time.

Once they are on board, Young Hunt says, "We should get out of here right now," but Broadhurst says no, they would only be ordered back and the people would think even less of them for having run.

They perform their tests as the fishermen watch from the wharf, the plant workers and their children from the beach, waiting for a verdict based on a process of which they must not have the first hint of an understanding, waiting to see if, because of the mysteriously arrived at findings of these inspectors, they will be allowed to sell the fish they have spent days catching or will have to dump them. Surely they must know their fish is bad. But they are not interested in how, by looking at it through a microscope, you can tell to what degree fish has broken down, or how many more microorganisms it has per gram than is allowed by regulations cooked up elsewhere.

He is not much interested in it either, but it is his job to investigate such things and take action on his findings.

Young Hunt says they should give the fish a passing grade and clear out while they can. "Who would ever know?" he says. News that a catch or a plant has been condemned is never taken well, but this bunch, he says, is the hardest-looking crowd he's ever seen.

The fish gets a failing grade in every category.

"This plant is closed as of right now," says Broadhurst, after they climb back onto the wharf.

"For how long?" says the manager.

"For as long as it takes to bring it up to standard," says Broadhurst.

"You're putting these people out of work," the manager says.

"Better to put people out of work than to poison them with rotten fish," says Broadhurst. "You'll have to dump all the fish in the plant and any caught today."

"This plant stays open," the manager says.

Broadhurst tells him that on his orders, no fish will be accepted from this plant at any market on the island, so they can stay open until doomsday if they want to. However, if he does not close down the plant, he will have his licence revoked and he will be arrested.

"Arrested by who?" the manager says.

"By the RCMP on orders from me," says Broadhurst.

"He says our fish are no good!" the manager shouts.

One of the plant workers knocks out of Young Hunt's hand the helmet he is still holding to his face.

"Is there something we can do to change your minds?" the manager says.

Whether this is a veiled threat or the offer of a bribe he isn't sure.

Broadhurst shakes his head.

"He says we have to dump the fish!" the manager shouts. The crowd erupts.

In the shouting he makes out the words "townies," "traitors" and "Canadians." There is no contradiction for these people, despite having voted for Confederation, denouncing feds as "Canadians." By Canadian, they do not mean confederate, they simply mean outsider, a kind of hyper-townie.

"This man used to be a fisherman like you," Young Hunt says, pointing at him. "He's one of you." There are scornful snorts of laughter. He would tell Young Hunt to shut up except he knows that they would seize on any sign of division between the members of the crew who would lose what little authority they still have left.

There is nothing he wants less than to be thought of as someone who "used to be a fisherman," the legitimizing member of this "fink force," as they are known along the coast. Someone who used to be an anti-confederate now walking around in what he still thinks of as his country with the badge of the federal Fisheries of Canada plastered on both shoulders. Someone who used to be a fisherman but now is a civil servant, getting paid to scrutinize and criticize the way that fishermen like his father and the ones he grew up with go about their work.

"He worked in a fish plant too," Young Hunt says. "This man can split a fish faster than anyone I've ever seen." This is true, if only because before this trip Young Hunt has never seen a fish split in his life.

"What if we don't let you go?" the manager says. "There's only one way out of here, and we can block it off just like that."

Some shout their support of this remark. "We should dunk them off the wharf," says the man who knocked Young Hunt's helmet from his hands.

A big man wearing rubber overalls and a yellow oilskin raincoat steps in front of the manager. "Go on," he says, dismissing them with a wave of his hand. "Go on, get out of here. Go on home before someone gets hurt."

The crowd falls silent.

The men of the *Belle Bay* turn around and make slowly for the boat.

The people cheer as if they believe that by this retreat of the inspectors, the matter of their fish plant has been settled and outsiders will never interfere with them again.

"*Go on!*" the man roars behind them.

Young Hunt runs. Broadhurst and Manning pick up the pace. He'll be damned if he'll show them he's scared. He feels something hit him between the shoulder blades and turns around. At his feet lies one small fish.

"A fish for the fisherman," a woman says. This is met with great guffaws.

He turns around and is hit again, this time just below the backside. Soon they are pelting him with fish from the catch they condemned. Broadhurst and Manning run, Broadhurst shouting, "You'll all be arrested for assault!"

He keeps walking and they follow just a few feet behind him, hurling fish with all their might. Some of the fish hit him with such force that he is driven forward and almost falls. When he reaches the wharf, he climbs down the ladder to the boat, where Broadhurst helps him aboard and closes the door behind him.

Fish hit the boat, thud on the roof, splatter against the windows, leaving trails of blood.

"You all right?" says Broadhurst.

He goes to his bunk, takes off his soiled clothing and lies down.

FOR PART OF my father's stint on the *Belle Bay*, we lived on the edge of Forest Pond, by pure chance in the summer house of Major Cashin's brother, a house that the legendary Major must have visited or even stayed in overnight.

My father, in talking about the house with his brothers or with neighbours, referred to it as "Cashin's."

"We'll be staying at Cashin's until May," he said, as if it was the Major's house.

This memory for some reason makes me feel the way I did in the first months of my adolescence: on summer nights when it was calm, trout breached in such numbers they registered like raindrops on the pond.

It was in this house that I picked up from my father my mania for weather watching. He had acquired it on his *Belle Bay* expeditions, partly out of necessity and partly out of boredom; it was important while on the water to listen frequently to forecasts and note changes in temperature and wind direction and velocity, and learn how to predict the weather from the mere look of the water and the sky.

In the evening, I listened to the *Fishermen's Broadcast* on CBC radio and later at night to the island-wide "temperature roundup." I took the radio into my room with me and, ignoring my brothers' complaints about the noise, listened to it in the dark. Every evening there was the same cold-shiver-inducing litany of south-coast place names: Burgeo, Fortune, Hermitage. I imagined myself looking out to sea at night from the window of a house in Hermitage, a house where there was never more than one light burning.

I was of course especially interested in what the weather was like along the south coast while my father was away. The *Fishermen's Broadcast* included a weather forecast for both the coastal communities and the fishing grounds, the various "banks," each of which I imagined as an expansive swell of water somehow clearly defined from all the others.

The latter were especially interesting, for the *Belle Bay* often did not put into port until late at night and sometimes, if the weather was too rough for docking, not at all. There were several broadcasters, one voice giving way to the next as the forecast moved around the island.

In spite of having seen the *Belle Bay*, I didn't fret for my father's safety, didn't think it a real possibility that he would not return. But there was nothing like thinking of him out there, the lights of the *Belle Bay* glowing in the dark like those of the radio transistors that I could see by looking through the perforated panel on the back. Often the radio crackled with static and the voices were very faint, as if the signal were being sent by short-wave from some stormbound Arctic hut.

"Winds light, west southwest, ten knots gusting to fifteen knots. Increasing rapidly to winds east, southeast, thirty knots gusting to fifty knots by midnight. Gale warning in effect." There were almost always advisories or warnings of some kind. A warning was more serious than an advisory. I knew the wind-warnings scale: small craft, gale force, storm force, hurricane force. The advisories were always perfunctorily announced in a "purely for your information" kind of way. Mind you, storm warnings were only slightly less perfunctorily announced, as if the announcers had been chosen on the basis of having voices least likely to cause undue or even entirely justified alarm. They droned eerily on as if the forecasts were being read by a succession of hermits who had long since lost interest in the outside world.

In the winter, there were often freezing-spray warnings. Freezing spray was water blown from the crests of waves onto ships, where it froze instantly. My father said that freezing spray made the *Belle Bay* look like a floating ice sculpture and often so increased her weight that she rode several feet lower than normal in the water and sometimes almost sank. He never spared us the details of the hazards of his trips, nor did my mother ever urge him to, at least not in front of us.

The forecasts for the banks seemed especially dramatic. "Seas ten feet, increasing to seas twenty to thirty feet by midnight and to seas forty feet by dawn." I curled up warm beneath my blankets and thought of my father out there where the voice on the radio made it sound so remote, a radio world accessible only via the *Belle Bay*, where it was always dark and there was always freezing spray, and nameless rime-encrusted small craft bobbed about unmanned, unseen.

"Forecast for the south coast including the Argentia, Belleoram, Burin, Grand Banks, Fortune, Harbour Breton, Hermitage, Hare Bay, Grey River, Ramea, Ramea Islands, Burgeo and Channel–Port aux Basques banks."

Ramea was off the southwest coast on Northwest Island, one of the Ramea Islands, a small archipelago that also included Big Island, Southwest Island, Harbour Island and Grepe Island. All except Big Island had been completely deforested by settlers since the nineteenth century, bald islands on which nothing grew, the topsoil either unable to rise to the challenge of a second growth from scratch or burned off by forest fires altogether. A ferry connected the unimaginably isolated Ramea to the unimaginably isolated Burgeo on the coast.

My father took photographs of the places they went to on the *Belle Bay*, and I remember especially well one that he took of Ramea: a man stands on a height of land; behind and below him is a harbour strewn with dories, an anachronistic pair of tall-masted schooners side by side; on the land beyond the harbour are scatterings of square, flat-roofed two-storey houses; and beyond the island the headlands of another island, partially obscured by mist.

MY FATHER TOLD me once that the smell of a beach is not the smell of the sea. Once you have gone far enough from land, the sea doesn't smell of anything except salt water, he said, water a hundred times saltier than blood. It isn't that the smell of salt is masking other smells. There *are* no other smells. This is why, unless you happen to be seasick, food cooked at sea smells and tastes so good. The body, for so long deprived of it, craves sensation. After your first prolonged stay at sea, you smell things back on land that you never smelled before, things you thought had no smell. Rock, for instance. He said that the first thing you smell on approaching Newfoundland by boat is rock. You smell it and even faintly taste it, a coppery metallic taste at the back of your mouth.

My father, just back home after three weeks on the *Belle Bay*, walked around as though in a daze, eyes on the ground as though he were searching for something. He stood at the fence in the backyard, his hand on the rail, and simply stared at the proliferous landscape, as if it were all brand-new to him.

It was not just smells and sights but sounds too — birds chirping, dogs barking, cars going by on the road outside the house, the distant whine of a power saw or, from some-where far off in the valley beyond the ridge, a rifle shot. The sound he missed most, he said, was the sound of the wind in the trees, the rustle of the topmost leaves as a land breeze moved among them.

He walked. What a novel sensation it must have been for him to walk, to propel himself more than a boat's length in one direction and feel the earth hard and motionless beneath his feet.

He walked up the road at a clip with no destination in mind. "I'm getting my land legs back," he said when he returned hours later.

The first couple of nights in his stationary bed he could not sleep — not that he minded much, for it simply allowed him to revel that much longer in idleness and in being back home, in not being on the water.

When he did sleep, he slept as he had not since he was last on land, before he set sail on the *Belle Bay*. A night at sea was at best one long dwall for him, a slumberous sleep during which his mind raced and he was always at least dimly aware of his surroundings and circumstances.

Even in winter, he spent as much of his week off as he could outdoors, shovelling snow, cutting a path in the driveway much wider than was necessary, pausing about every other shov-elful to look around or relight a cigarette.

When my father was home from his trips, my weather-watching habits did not change much. He had become, from his time on the *Belle Bay*, an obsessive tapper of barometers. He couldn't pass by one without tapping it. We always had a func-tional barometer in the house, and often more than one. My father would cringe when the barometer registered a sudden drop in air pressure, and he knew bad weather was coming, as if it put him back on the *Belle Bay*, as if even during his time home he was vicariously on board with whoever rode on the *Belle Bay* when it was not his shift.

He would not sleep while a storm was raging, for the sounds of the storm were incorporated into his sea dreams and made them that much worse.

There was nothing I would rather do than watch a storm, so I kept vigil with him throughout the night, he sitting through hours of self-induced, nightmare-preventing sleeplessness, reading *The Reader's Digest* or doing crossword puzzles while sipping on a rye and ginger ale, while I, with my face to the window, kept him informed on the progress of the storm. "For God's sake, Wayne, get away from the window," he said, as if by watching it I was encouraging the storm, as if unless it was ignored it would never peter out.

Sometimes in spite of a storm he did go to sleep and spent the night thrashing about and shouting instructions to the skipper or one of the *Belle Bay* bunch while my mother lay sleepless beside him, afraid to wake him, for he always came roaring out of a nightmare when touched or spoken to as if such a prompt brought him in his dream to the brink of death, as if it sank the *Belle Bay* the last remaining inch below the waves.

Telephones were rare in the outports, so when my father was away, his only means to call home was the ship-to-shore telephone. We got about half an hour's warning from federal Fisheries that the call was coming, as it had to be patched through to our phone by some complicated series of connections.

We took turns talking to him. The line crackled with static and his voice was very faint. He sounded as if he were calling from under water.

We had to say "Over" each time we stopped to let him speak, which we boys thought was great fun but my mother hated. While we fought among ourselves over what order we should talk to him in, each of us wanting to go last so that we could say "Over and out," my mother walked about arms folded, smoking, swearing that she was fed up with having conversations with her husband as if the two of them were in the Navy, having to say "Over" every fifteen seconds. But she always spoke to him.

Fearful that by not calling he would give away the fact that he had been drinking, he was most faithful about calling when he was least able to pretend that he was sober.

"You sound pretty pleased with yourself, over," my mother would say, a code phrase she need not have bothered with — we knew what it meant. He protested his sobriety, but there was no fooling her.

Her tone starting out would be reproachful, but perhaps because of having to say "Over" at the end of every sentence, rolling her eyes as she did so, she wound up laughing or making kisses into the phone as she never did when he was sober. My mother would make a long, drawn out smooching noise, then say, "Over," bursting into giggles, then into gales of laughter when my father did the same. "Other people can hear this call you know, over," she'd say.

"Where are you calling from, Dad, over?" I asked him. When he told me — Roddicton, Inglee, English Harbour — I wrote it down so that later I could find it on the map.

"I'm stormbound, Wayne, over."

"So are we. We're stuck in the house. Are you on the *Belle Bay* now? Over."

"Yes. We're tied up at the wharf in Ramea, over."

I could picture it, the *Belle Bay* moored and bobbing, my father's view of Ramea like that of someone on a trampoline.

"My God, Wayne," he said once, his voice suddenly breaking with emotion. "What a country we could have been. What a country we were one time."

I fell silent. My mother took the phone from me, went out into the hall and closed the door.

"I know," I heard my mother say. "We still are, sweetheart. I know. Try not to think about it, now. Don't be by yourself, all right? Stay with the others."

If they were docked and it was too rough to stay on board the *Belle Bay*, they found whatever accommodations they could. There were no hotels, bed and breakfasts or even boarding houses in most of the places they made port. If they were lucky, a priest or minister would take them in, or old couples who, because their children had moved away, had rooms not slept in for years. Otherwise, they displaced children from their beds, or slept on sofas, waking in the morning as a family of strangers began its day around them in self-conscious silence. The members of the crew would venture out from their various houses after breakfast and find some shed or flakehouse where they could pass the day together smoking and drinking the rum they had brought in case of such a stranding.

Newfoundland is at the end of the line weather-wise, the last stop for storms that come across the continent or up the Atlantic seaboard from the Gulf of Mexico. And stop they often do, especially in winter, giant low-pressure systems remaining stationary, generating northeast winds and snow that lasts for days. Night after night, a large encircled L appears in exactly the same place on the television weather map, the weatherman sheepishly explaining why, despite his predictions to the contrary, the storm has not moved on.

I remember my mother nervously smoking as she listened. She regarded the weatherman, Bob Lewis, with a kind of skeptical dread, owing to the inaccuracy of his forecasts. It was as though he was a symptom of some larger chaos that caused things to happen without reason or forewarning. "He can't forecast the days of the week," she said, staring at him on the screen as he described the track he believed some storm would take. But she watched him anyway. His forecasts, even if they were little more than fiction, gave to her anxiety some shape and substance.

We gathered round the set and watched with her, waiting for the L's to turn up on the map. It seemed that as soon as my father left on one of his trips, those L's popped up everywhere. Even if there had been none on the entire map of the continent the day before, there were swarms of them the next.

Troughs too shallow to be designated lows deepened as the *Belle Bay* headed west. Within their zones of influence, the barometric pressure dropped, the isobars of each low compressed to a vortex of concentric shapes.

Clipper storms stacked up like airplanes from east to west, destination Newfoundland; Gulf of Mexico storms hugged the coast until they plowed into the current south of Sable Island, banked off it and wildly veered northeast. The storms crossed three peninsulas, the Burin, the Avalon, the Bonavista, then stalled, brought up solid fifty miles off the northeast coast as if a mooring line with fifty miles of slack had at last run out. With the ocean to provide them with an endless source of moisture and the wind off the ice pack making sure the snow would never change to rain, there was theoretically no reason why they could not last forever.

For me, the map was a representation not of space but time. It was a time grid whose various sections could just as easily have been numbered as named, for the names meant nothing to me. The provinces and states, whose existence I did not really believe in, were preconfigurations of the next few days, the moods that would prevail in the house. The past was off-screen right, the future off-screen left and the picture on the screen was a photograph of now. Here comes next week, there goes last week. It was easy to imagine that the past was recoverable, that you could pull it back like a ticker tape, and across the screen would go the L's and H's that in code contained the past.

I imagined some giant L-shaped dirigible that would not move on until someone cut the rope by which it was moored to the island. Me trudging off through the storm, wading blindly through snowdrifts until I somehow found the rope that was thicker than a tree trunk and hacked at it with my axe until it broke and the ragged end of it trailed off across the snow as the storm withdrew.

My father was in some nebulous, electronic otherworld, in the phone, in the wind-whipped telephone wires, in the dust-covered workings of the radio, in the warm transistor tubes, in the worm-like filaments of orange light that dimmed and flickered when the wind was at its height.

He was wherever the voices on the air came from. He had not gone anywhere in space. He had been transported to this world of strange-sounding high-pitched voices in which storms of static raged like blizzards. He was out there somewhere in air as thick with static as a blizzard was with snow. And he was tenuously, invisibly there on the television weather map of Newfoundland. "That's where your father is spending the night," my mother said, pointing to some jagged little inlet or peninsula west of Baie d'Espoir, and often pointing to it the next night and the next, while on the screen Bob Lewis pointed elsewhere.

If the place where my father was stranded was big enough, Bob Lewis might say what temperature it was there now and with his marker write the number on the corresponding section of the map. It was twenty-two degrees Fahrenheit in Ramea. That was all the verification of its existence we would get.

Sometimes in the middle of the night, the phone would ring, and I would hear my mother run to answer it. A crank call. A wrong number. Nothing on the other end but dial tone. She went to bed again in the vain hope of getting back to sleep. I would hear the click of her lighter and, soon after, smell the smoke of a cigarette.

During the worst winter storms, when she was especially anxious or upset and before it became impossible to go outside, she took us to spend the night at her parents' house, which my father referred to as "the world's most mournful dwelling place."

My grandparents, though they had electricity, used low-watt bulbs that lit the house about as brightly as oil lanterns used to do. The place was always dim and full of looming shadows that went up the wall and partway across the ceiling. Whenever we came to visit, my grandfather, knowing that we never said it otherwise, insisted that we join them in the kitchen to say the rosary. I couldn't help feeling that we were praying for my father's safe return.

My grandfather had spent at least half of every day from age ten to thirty-five fishing for cod off Petty Harbour, and he playfully teased my mother for being so worried about what, compared with the storms he said he had made his way through in a dory powered by nothing more than his arms and a pair of oars, was "barely a breeze."

I imagined him "sou'westered" as he called it, dressed in gleaming oilskin from head to toe, plying his absurdly tiny, inadequate craft up and down the sides of massive, slate-black waves.

The wind surged against the side of the house, the window panes buckled inward and the whistle in the wood stove rose to a shriek until the gust subsided, at which point my grandfather would look up from the paper he was reading and, wetting his thumb to turn a page, say, "Barely a breeze, Genevieve, barely a breeze, my dear."

It worked for a while. My mother would laugh at his teasing, encourage him. Then, when he saw she was past the point that his stories would do her any good, he went to bed while we boys were sent to watch TV with the sound turned down so low we had to sit within a foot of it to hear it.

My mother sat with her mother in the kitchen, the two of

them talking softly, my grandmother reassuring my mother that the storm raging outside was not as bad as it looked — she had seen storms much worse before, and my father was doubtless safe on shore.

He was never more conspicuously absent than on those nights we spent in the world's most mournful dwelling place and from the kitchen came the murmur of voices while in the front room of the wind-besieged house my brothers and I huddled by the TV set, trying to hear, above the storm, some program like *The Big Valley* or *Bonanza*.

Some summer evenings while my father was away, my mother piled us into the car and drove us down the road to Maddox Cove. We followed the flume into Petty Harbour, where the roads are so narrow it's necessary for a car to pull onto the shoulder to let another one go by.

The Catholic side, where my mother's parents had lived until they set out for the Goulds in the early 1900s, was on our right. Above the Protestant side on our left was the entrance to a long-abandoned mine, a dark door-shaped hole bored straight into the cliff. As a child, my grandmother had been warned not to cross the bridge to the Protestant side of town lest she be spirited away into the mine that led directly down to hell by "blacks," as the Catholics called the Protestants.

Beyond the breakwater, pink buoys marked the site of lobster traps. Fishing nets with large cork floats attached were spread out on the ground to dry. Dories being painted or repaired lay overturned beside the road. There were dozens of dories and skiffs anchored inside the breakwater, all linked by an elaborate network of ropes that kept them from colliding when the wind came up. Here, the water was like that of the pond below our house, so calm it mirrored the pattern of lights on the westside hill. But beyond the seawall, there were lozenge-like ripples on the water, the closest thing to calm the ocean that far from shore could get.

Maddox Cove is just up the shore from Petty Harbour. It's sparsely settled, just half a dozen houses on the north side of the cove that are owned by fishermen who moor their boats in Petty Harbour. There are no wharves, no breakwater, just an open, unprotected harbour, a horizon uncluttered by jutting rocks or islands, clear sailing all the way to the Old World.

We picked among the beach rocks for the remains of various shallow-water sea creatures that had been stranded by the tide. Sea urchins, crabs, tom cods, sculpins, jellyfish, even capelin, the last of which had washed ashore two months ago. We found cables of kelp, still wet, encrusted with little sea snails, and long tentacles of seaweed.

While we combed the beach for "skimmers," flat rocks that when thrown properly skipped along the surface of the water, my mother walked off by herself on the wet, wave-rippled sand near the water, her hands in the pockets of her jacket, her bandana tied beneath her chin. At a certain distance from us she stopped and looked out to sea.

I imagined that being at the sea's edge made her feel closer to my father, made her miss him less, or miss him more but in a way that felt good, as missing him sometimes made me feel.

Petty Harbour was not home for her the way Ferryland still was for my father, in spite of it being the birthplace of her parents. She had never lived there. By coming here, she was getting away from home, away from things that reminded her of him. Except us. And the sea, of course. There was no getting away from that.

The sea reminded her of where he was, but the beach, aside from costing nothing to visit and keeping us children endlessly occupied without much need of supervision, was a place where no one bearing bad news could call her on the phone or come by the house.

Once, as she was coming back down the beach, it was clear from her red-rimmed eyes that she'd been crying.

"What's wrong, Mom?" I said.

"Nothing's wrong," she said.

"Mom?" I said.

The others were out of earshot.

"What?"

"Do you know what happened on the beach?"

"What beach?" she said. "This beach?" She didn't sound as if she was hiding something.

"To Dad," I said. "On the beach in Ferryland. When he was going off to college. Before he went. I think him and his father were on the beach or something. Did something happen?"

"My love, I don't know what you mean," she said.

I saw that it was true. She didn't know.

"Never mind," I said. "I thought Dad said something happened, but maybe I got it mixed up."

I knew she would ask my father if he had put this idea in my head. And I knew that he would tell her no.

We went back to the others. She sat down on the beach rocks. We sat down with her, four boys suddenly, solemnly well behaved, fearfully watching her, dreading another loss of control, another sign that she was more than just our mother and had secret sorrows of her own.

There had been other times like this, times when in his absence she disappeared into her room for hours, or walked up the cartroad to the top of her father's farm. When she reappeared, her eyes were puffy from crying, though we never acknowledged it, never asked her what was wrong. We assumed that at the bottom of it all was this job of his, his long absences from home, the anxiety, the loneliness. We were partly right. But how exactly these things manifested themselves between them they hid from us as best they could.

We stayed there until past twilight, sitting on the beach rocks with our mother while she smoked, all of us facing seaward as if we were waiting for a boat to come ashore.

There was still no wind, but it was getting cold. She shivered.

"Snuggle up, boys," she said. It had been ages since she had asked us to. We used to "snuggle up" with her on Saturday mornings while my father cooked us breakfast. She took Brian on her lap. I knelt behind her and put my arms around her neck, rested my chin on her shoulder, and Ken and Craig, flanking her, each took one of her arms.

"Is everybody warm?" she said. We nodded. "Me too," she said.

Off to our left, above the hills behind the Brow, we could see in the sky the faint glow of St. John's, five miles of woods away. By boat, Ferryland was thirty miles south, ten miles closer than by road. Far out on the water, beyond the eastern point of Maddox Cove, came the periodic flash of the lighthouse at Cape Spear.

Every so often, as if the sea had shrugged it ashore, an almost silent swell broke on the beach.

"This is nice, hey?" she said. Brian said we should stay there all night. My mother laughed and kissed him on the top of the head. "We'll go camping when your Dad gets back," she said. "All of us, all night, okay?" Brian, who never forgot a promise, nodded.

We stayed a little longer, until my mother declared that it was time to head home. We left, scrambling over beach rocks that we couldn't see and that slid crazily about beneath our feet so that we had to hold on to each other to keep from falling, my mother shrieking with laughter as the four of us all but dragged her to the road. When we reached the car, I looked up. The sky was full of stars.

By THE SEVENTIES, there were no more gatherings at Uncle Harold's house. With all the children grown up, there was not enough room for everyone. The family no longer made the monthly drive to Ferryland, not even in summer, though now the road was paved. My parents went only once or twice a year, when it was my father's turn to tend his parents' graves.

You could go only so long remaining righteous in defeat, protesting that your having lost did not change the fact that you were right, that it was the so-called winners who had lost, because what they had won was not worth winning. Most anti-confederates found some face-saving way of getting on with it.

My father, however, still saw himself as a man without a country. He knew it struck many people as ridiculous, but this, far from discouraging him, only seemed to egg him on and give him some sort of perverse satisfaction. It was as though he courted scorn, as though, the world being what it was, the mark of his true worth was that it didn't take him seriously.

He did not seek converts to his point of view, always found some way of distinguishing himself from other people who still professed to be anti-confederates. He sniffed with derision when I told him once of a man I had heard of who, every April 1, wore a black armband. No one else's anti-confederacy was wholly genuine as far as my father was concerned. He dismissed out of hand any supposed anti-confederate who wasn't old enough to remember what Newfoundland was like before Confederation.

"Take away his unemployment insurance," my father said, "and see how quick he'll change his mind."

He still reserved his greatest scorn for the "closet confederates," who he said were going about staging phony protests, having the hypocritical temerity to have voted for Confederation and now to be going round on April 1, wearing black armbands, badges, pins.

One night, as we were sitting at the kitchen table after all the rest had gone to bed, I told him that the only way you could know for certain that people were closet confederates was if they admitted to it. And why would anyone do that?

He told me there was one other way that you could know. When I asked him to explain, he shook his head.

"Come on, what's the other way?" I said.

"Never mind," he said.

I asked him if anyone who campaigned for independence had ever confessed to him to voting for Confederation.

"Never mind," he said, "never mind," as if I had had my chance, as if, by missing the hint that he had given me, I had shown myself to be unworthy of some secret.

"I think if you're going to talk about closet confederates, you should prove that they exist," I said. "Why don't you tell me who they are?"

"They know who they are," he said.

I told him that his was the animating myth of many Newfoundlanders, the myth that the true king was always in exile or in rags while some pretender held the throne.

"If you say so," he said, but smiling fondly at me in a way that made me feel even younger and more naive than I was.

I understood now that the anti-confederates had risked more, infinitely more, than the confederates, who, if they had lost the referendum, would no doubt have gone on to fight another one someday, and another one, ad infinitum, for unlike Newfoundland, the country they were fighting for would always be there. (Or so it must have seemed then.)

For them there would always have been hope, if nothing else. Not so the anti-confederates, who, if they lost once, would be defeated for all time. Perhaps they, Charlie Johnston, my father, his brothers, my mother's family, hadn't understood this until it was too late.

Symbolic of all of them was Peter Cashin, who had hung on in the legislature after 1949, still arguing against Confederation as if he thought the referendum had been just another election, the results of which, in four years, could be overturned. It had taken years for him to realize that the battle he was fighting was long since lost.

He eventually settled for a sinecure from Joey Smallwood, who wanted to appease his half of Newfoundland as much as possible. He was made director of Civil Defence, head of the Home Guard, Emergency Measures. Almost a figure of fun.

The Major.

"REMEMBER THE CATECHISMS, Wayne?" my father would often ask me when we talked about the past. He fondly recalled them as any father would a game that he and his son had fallen out of the habit of playing. Though to him they were more than just a game, the writing and reciting of them. He often wished that he had saved them and regretted that, as he put it, he had somehow lost the "knack" of writing them. When I was a boy, "the catechism" was a routine that we performed for visitors, as we had at the Come Home Year party. In the first catechisms, when I was four or five, my responses consisted mainly of simple sentences with one syllable words, and even then most of their meaning was lost on me, which seemed to be what tickled people most, me answering my father like some prodigy of irony when in fact I understood almost nothing I was saying. He sat on the chesterfield, I stood in front of him, and as solemnly as he asked his questions, I gave the answers he had helped me memorize.

Q: What, since 1949, have not tasted quite the same?
A: Blueberries.

Q: Very good. From what pastime do we derive less pleasure than we did in former days?

A: Trouting.

Q: Why is that?

A: The trout no longer jump into our boats. We have to catch them.

Q: Excellent. Is there a form of bliss that you will never know?

A: There are many.

Q: Foremost among them?

A: Ignorance of him who, toad-like, croaks and dwells among the undergrowth.

Q: Name him.

A: Joey Smallwood.

Q: Does he leave behind him as he goes a trail of slime?

A: He does.

Q: Do we fear him?

A: We do not.

Q: Scorn him?

A: Yes. With all our hearts we do.

Q: Does he, pretender, occupy the throne?

A: He does.

Q: Has he who will displace him yet come into the world?

A: He has.

Q: In what most favoured region of the country does he dwell?

A: Avalon.

Q: Is he known to us?

A: Perhaps.

Q: He knows his destiny?

A: Not yet.
Q: Who might he be?
A: He might be anyone. He might be me.

THE ENEMY WAS "Joey."

It seems I always knew that. I knew it before I started school.

He was a barely personified agency of opposition, the "thwart," my father called him, the nebulous something that we Johnstons were against. He existed only on movie screens, or in the television set, which was turned off the instant he appeared. About the nature of his threat to us I was never certain. We would have changed the channel, except the only other one we could get was the CBC, and the utter worthlessness of anything Canadian was for us an article of faith.

So the instant we saw Joey's face, someone ran to the set and turned it off. *"Joey!"* the first of us to see him would shout, alerting the one nearest to the set, sounding the alarm. Even when our parents weren't watching, we children did it. About their aversion to Joey they were so sincere that to avoid him seemed to us the grown-up thing to do.

To us, he was a bow-tie wearing despot, who by the time I started school had been ruling Newfoundland for fifteen years. He was regarded with a mixture of terror and scornful amusement. He was the only premier Newfoundland had had since Confederation. Confederation had entered the world with Joey; he had led Newfoundlanders to it and tempted them to partake of it as surely as the serpent had led Eve to the apple. And we had thereby fallen from a state of grace that could never be recovered, been banished forever from the paradise of independence.

He won elections by landslides, despite an almost unbroken record of spectacular failures, treasury-draining economic development schemes, the hope of whose improbable success he clung to long after it was certain even to his closest friends that they were doomed.

No matter what the implications might be for us as Newfoundlanders, we delighted in the failures of Joey's debt-defying schemes. He was like a tightrope walker who never managed a single successful walk but kept raising the rope higher and higher, in the end trying to perform from the greatest height while wrapped from head to toe in bandages and with every limb encumbered by a cast.

During the first fifteen years of Joey's reign, Newfoundland went from the solvency of a $45 million surplus to a several-billion-dollar debt. It was an epic debt, ludicrously huge in proportion to our population of less than half a million.

It was vindication of sorts. Confederation might be here to stay, though no one ever said so in so many words, but it had all backfired on Joey in a manner that was no less gratifying for bringing with it the complete ruination of Newfoundland.

During the last of Joey's days in office, the Johnstons refused to risk heartbreak by even considering the possibility that they would finally be rid of him.

"He'll worm his way out of this one yet, you just watch," my uncle Harold said. "This one" was the deadlocked election of October 1971. Strange things happened in Newfoundland politics during the next six months. Politicians who were offered cabinet posts to do so switched parties, crossing the House of Assembly from both sides, the balance of power teetering back and forth. Joey's government at one point had fewer members than the opposition, but he somehow managed to forestall a vote of non-confidence and stayed in power.

"It's the referendum all over again," Aunt Eva declared. "The whole thing is fixed."

But Joey announced his resignation on January 13, 1972, at four o'clock in the afternoon, as it was getting dark. I was fourteen and just home from high school in St. John's. His speech, which he delivered from his office, was carried live on TV and radio. Life in Newfoundland came to a standstill. In many homes throughout the province that night, people wept and swore bitterly at the ungratefulness of those Newfoundlanders who had voted against him. As in the referendum of 1948, about half of them had. A quarter of a century later, the country was once again split down the middle.

There was neither weeping nor swearing in our house. Harold and Marg and Eva and Jim came by in the evening.

"It's a happy night in heaven," Eva said.

"Yes, I suppose it is," my father said.

They all said it was a shame that Nan Johnston and Mr. Charlie and Freda could not have lived to see this day.

For a while they were silent. It sounded as if a coup were under way outside, so many shotguns were being fired off in celebration, in mocking mimicry of what the confederates had done on referendum night twenty-four years earlier. Joey had not only given us the satisfaction of defeating him but had bowed out about as ungracefully as it was possible to do, prolonging his reign long past the point where everyone but him knew he was finished. Eva, sipping on a drink, swore the suspense had been such that she had foresworn TV, radio and newspapers for weeks. "My God," she said, putting her hand on her chest, "I thought that man would never go."

They decided to call the Ferryland Johnstons, Gordon and Kitty and Millie. As each of them took a turn on the phone, their voices changed instantly, as if they had placed a call to the past, as if they were looking out the kitchen window of the old house at the lighthouse on the Head, looking out across the Downs, which at night were always a shade darker than the water.

Ferryland, Gordon told them, was going wild. Fireworks. Bands of merrymakers going by on the road below the house, motorcades of cars honking. Guns going off. Though it was a clear night, the foghorn in the lighthouse had been sounding since four o'clock. Gordon doubted that anyone in Ferryland would get to sleep that night. It was as if Confederation had been undone.

But they spoke not with rancour or with vehemence or even, after a while, with vindictive glee, but wistfully. Something had ended, something more than just Joey's reign as premier. It was hard to say just what, but something had. And harder still to imagine what would take its place.

However things might have been in Ferryland, the celebration in the Goulds did not go on all night or even until midnight. In our house, by ten o'clock, the Johnstons were subdued, reflective.

"We're still stuck with Confederation, but at least we've seen the last of Joey Smallwood," Eva said. The others murmured their assent.

They must have thought that with Joey gone, they could at last, if not reconcile themselves to Confederation, then forget about it, not be daily reminded by his face and his voice and his name in the paper of their father's Old Lost Land.

It had not occurred to them that they might miss this last link with the battle, that they had in part defined themselves by their opposition to Joey, that to rail against him was a way of sustaining the illusion that Confederation might still somehow be undone.

They had all been in their twenties when the fight for Newfoundland was lost, young men and women. Defeat came as an intervention. They had lost not something they had merely hoped would last but something they had had no reason to think they would ever lose.

Now, in their early fifties, they were no less bewildered than they had been back then. They had followed the river of what should have been, knowing it led nowhere.

WHEN MY FATHER had put in enough years on the south-coast run to quit if he wanted to, he did. He worked now in a federal Fisheries laboratory that had been part of the U.S. Army base in the Second World War at Pleasantville, St. John's, a place of converted barracks and dormitories and squat three-storey wooden buildings constructed by the Americans for a war that, for all they knew, would last for decades.

That science could not save or even much improve the fisheries he had by this time known for years. He performed on a rote basis quality-control tests on samples of fish collected around the island by younger men who told him he had no idea what their lives were like. He became so adept at it that he could think of other things or even think of nothing while he worked. It seemed to him sometimes that he was the opposite of everything he wished to be. All he wanted was to spend his days outdoors, away from microscopes, Bunsen burners, beakers, test tubes.

My father and his brothers, almost every morning from the age of ten, fished for hours with their father before they started school, as much part-time fishermen as he was. When they came back into the Pool and landed their catch, they walked down the road to the schoolhouse past Most Holy Trinity Church on the landward side of the road, and their father went up the hill to the forge behind his house and began his other job. They had all been working for five hours by the time the school bell rang at nine o'clock.

He had not been at sea for seven years, had not been fishing for thirty, but my father shaped his day like the fisherman he once was, rising every morning he was able to at four o'clock, the time his father used to wake him and his brothers in the years they spent together on the water. At no time of the year was the sun up at four in the morning. Every day began in darkness. It was important to him that it did. It was important to him that he not begin his day getting ready for work, that work he disliked not be his reason for rising when he did. He had at least that much control, was to that degree at least not fatefully bound by his ill-chosen profession.

Then, too, there were the dreams he had. For some reason, he had his worst dreams when he slept past four o'clock. He told me that he dreamed of his father. Sometimes that he and his father and brothers were about to wreck on Ferryland Head, which they had many times come close to doing. He dreamed of the time he and his father lost the sled when they were cutting ice, when he walked for hours not knowing that his spleen was ruptured. My father, lost in the dark wood of his dreams, called out to his father while my mother lay beside him, trying as gently as possible to coax him into wakefulness, whispering his name. "Art, Art, wake up." He always woke with a start, the bed shaking as if he had just dropped into it from some great height.

I was eighteen, attending college in St. John's. Every morning when I got up I found him standing at the kitchen window, the day for him already hours old. He loved to have the house to himself when it was dark outside. Wearing slacks but barefoot and shirtless, he would lean on the kitchen counter, side-on, just to the right of the sink into which he tipped the ashes of his cigarettes as he looked out the window, waiting for the first lightening of the sky above the Shoal Bay Hills, watching the hills themselves come into view, a rolling horizon a shade darker than the sky above it. He stood there looking out the window for hours.

At seven o'clock, he started his day again and ours for the first time by turning on the radio, which was always tuned to the CBC. (Joey was gone, the CBC no longer off limits.) He listened to the marine forecast as if it still mattered to him how high the waves would be that day and what the chances were of freezing spray and when the tides would ebb and flow. He noted it all in his journal/log, was often still writing in it when we came out for breakfast. He kept a meteorological diary, and to his weather observations appended notes in ship's-log form throughout the day. "February 9, 1976. Snow flurries and drifting snow. Had to dig the car out. Snow with southeast winds expected by mid-afternoon, changing to rain overnight. Wayne home from school with flu. Because of storm, Mom taking day off too..."

He took an early retirement at the age of fifty-five. "The fish will soon be gone," he said, as if by way of explaining his retirement. He and his co-workers had been telling their superiors for years what the fishermen had been telling them. The fish would soon be gone. And perhaps their superiors had been telling *their* superiors. No one knew for certain. Nothing was done. And then one day — and it seemed to happen that suddenly — the fish *were* gone.

WHILE OUR LAST house, the only one we ever owned, was being built, we lived for six months across the road from it in my grandfather's house, the whole family sleeping in the room that my grandparents used to sleep in but that my grandfather abandoned for another, smaller one after my grandmother died. For six months, the seven of us, my parents, four teenage boys and my seven-year-old sister, slept and, for the most part, lived in that one room, the door of which was always closed. The rest of the house, except the kitchen and the bathroom, was practically off limits to us, even the living room, for we had to go to our bedroom when my grandfather retired to his at eight o'clock. The precious interval between dinner and bedtime we spent in a manner we were not accustomed to — saying the rosary, on our knees in the kitchen, leaning, beads in hand, on chairs or on the daybed.

It was deemed to be such an imposition on my grandfather, of whom everyone was terrified, to have the seven of us in his house, that my mother warned us not to make a peep once he went to his room. My parents slept in what must have been the bed my mother was conceived in, it looked so old, and the five of us children slept on the floor, between the foot of the bed and the wall, on our sides, for there was not enough room to sleep on our backs or on our stomachs. We undressed for bed in shifts, my parents first while we waited outside in the hall. Once they were under the covers they called my sister in, and when she was in her sleeping bag and facing the wall, we boys went in.

It seemed the house across the road would never be built. Our bedroom window faced it, and we spent a lot of time watching its progress from there. An old house on the site had to be torn down to make way for ours. It was one of the oldest houses in the Goulds, a white saltbox with a dark green trim. After it was levelled by a bulldozer, people were permitted to scavenge for firewood, and there was not much of it left to be hauled away when they were finished.

We moved into my grandfather's house in mid-October. The shell of our house, a small bungalow, was built very quickly, raising our hopes that the whole thing might be finished before spring. But work inside proceeded very slowly. Once the shell was up to protect them from the coming snow and hide them from the eyes of their employers across the road, the carpenters took their time. The winter was a bad one. One morning we woke up to see a snowdrift arced across what soon would be our front yard, cresting at about fifteen feet right where the driveway would be.

As soon as there was a floor solid enough to hold us, we went over there to walk around, not minding the dark. We were so glad to be on our own again, even if it was only for as long as we could stand the cold. I thought the place would always have the new-house smells of unfinished wood, gyproc, sawdust and cement. By the light of the flashlights we carried, we could see each other's breath. Though there were only joists to mark the rooms, we staked out our territory, the four of us boys sitting in what would be our room, staring enviously through the wooden uprights at my sister in her room; beyond hers was my parents' room, another set of uprights away, my father sitting on a sawhorse, smoking a cigarette, my mother with arms folded, staring out the window at her father's house across the road. It seemed to us the pinnacle of privacy.

The plasterboard went up, the pink insulation and the ceiling tiles, the doors. In April, carpet was put down throughout the house. The furnace and appliances were installed, as was the wiring. The last thing to be constructed, or assembled rather, was the fireplace. The variously coloured stones for it had been delivered months too early and had lain outside all winter, buried under mounds of snow, protected only by a canvas tarp and a plastic sheet. My father had fretted all winter about the stones, certain he would find them split into pieces by the frost in the spring. But when the stonemason removed the coverings, the stones were all intact, protected from the cold by the snow, he said, as if this had been his plan all along. The whole family watched him build the fireplace, artfully trowelling the massive granite stones into place with cement. When the large grey granite mantelpiece was put in place, the house was finished.

We had lived in some indescribably dilapidated houses, at best in old houses maintained to minimum standards. We spent a winter in one house that had no refrigerator. We put our perishables outside on the steps, losing everything except the milk to neighbourhood dogs. One Friday my father, determined not to be deprived for the umpteenth time of bacon and eggs for his Saturday morning breakfast, stayed up all night, keeping guard in the porch over his pound of bacon on the veranda. Each time the pack of dogs advanced on the house, my father chased them off with a shovel that he wielded like a battle-axe. This was 1965. In another house we all awoke one morning to find it being painted by strangers who had been hired by the landlord who had neglected to tell us not only that the painters were coming but that the place was up for sale and we had a week to find somewhere else to live. We lived in a house without running water, kept our drinking water in a bucket on the porch, where in the winter the first few inches froze and we had to break the ice with an axe before we filled our glasses. The water was delicious but so cold it gave us headaches. We lived in a house beside a tavern, and between the two there was not so much as a fence or a patch of grass. The patrons brawled almost nightly in the gravel parking lot while we watched from our upstairs bedroom windows. In the backyard of one house, sewage ran raw from a ruptured septic tank, bubbling up from the ground like oil. In another house, my father chopped clean off with a hatchet the head of a rat, having waited hours for him to emerge from the basement drainage pipe.

But in this house, this tiny house, everything was new. My memories of our first days in it are not spoiled by the fact that within a year it became almost mythically dysfunctional. Impossibly, blessedly, everything worked for a while.

August 1981

There is no way of saying goodbye to my father that will not remind him of the day on the beach in Ferryland when he and Charlie said goodbye. Not for a long time has he let slip a word about what happened on the beach, nor have I said anything about it. Whatever it is about Ferryland that has haunted him for years is caught up with that day and that goodbye. I know that much. But I am resigned to never knowing more.

Every goodbye since then has recalled that one for my father, and ours especially, because of all his children I am the one who most reminds him of his young self and so of his childhood. It is hard to say just why this is, but we both know it. I can see in my father's eyes that he is dreading our goodbye as much as I am. We must avoid being alone with each other so that he can simply be one of several who see me off at the airport with a handshake and best wishes. We have tacitly agreed to be vigilant and not be the last two at the dinner table or the first two up for breakfast. But the effect of all this is to keep the thought of encountering the other so constantly in mind that it seems bound to happen.

The day before I am supposed to leave, I go to the newsroom at the St. John's paper where I work to clear my desk of four years' worth of papers, letters, drafts of essays and short stories. I fancy there might be something worth preserving, so I pile it all into a box and put it in the car. Driving home, the box on the front seat beside me, I pick through it with one hand, and by the time I reach the Goulds I have decided that there is nothing worth keeping after all. I park in the driveway, remove the box and head for the trash barrel in the backyard. And when I turn the corner of the house, when I am close enough to the barrel that to turn away and make for the back door would be too transparent an attempt to avoid him, I see my father just as unmistakably headed for the barrel with an armload of flattened cardboard boxes and other things I cleared out of my room the day before.

I know, before he begins to speak, that he is going to tell me. Everything favours it. If he does not tell me now he never will. I am leaving. He knows I plan to be a writer. He knows, or hopes, that someday I will write about him. He cannot get the story straight in his mind and believes that when I tell it he will understand it better.

I do not know it yet, but there is a symmetry here that it would be pointless for us to resist. The time of the year is the same, early September, which in Newfoundland means early fall. Even the time of day is the same, almost twilight. The sun is low in the west, barely above the grove of spruce on the hill beside our house; on our backyard, on the meadows between it and the pond, on the pond and on the Shoal Bay Hills falls the same sad yellow light, the last light of a September day when the air is clear and, after sunset, quickly cools.

Years later I will wonder if my father saw me from the house making for the trash barrel and hurried out so we would meet, if there had been no tacit agreement between us to avoid each other and it was only me avoiding him and he thought I had done so long enough.

"Hello, Wayne," my father says.

"Hi, Dad." There is nothing I can do but meet him at the barrel.

"I thought I'd burn this tonight while there's no wind," he says. "There'll be a gale tomorrow night."

"Yeah?"

"Yes," my father says, as if he is sick to death of gales, though I know he will track the storm on his instruments and record the data in his book. "Southeast wind and rain. It's on its way."

And by the time it gets here, it occurs to me, I will be gone. A storm I will not be here to see will come in from Petty Harbour and above the Shoal Bay Hills. About this time tomorrow night, hours after the wind comes up, the first drops of rain will patter on the kitchen window and on the window of the room I have slept in almost every night for the past ten years. But there is no wind now, none. The pond is so calm it reflects the trees around it and the sky. And when the sun dips below the trees, the pond is like black glass. On its surface are reflected the lights of houses near the water and the street lamps on the poles around the pond.

"Let me get mine started first," he says. The thick cardboard will take longer to light and burn than what I have in the box. My father stuffs the barrel with cardboard, takes a sheet of paper from the box, lights it with a match, then drops it in. The cardboard catches. At first there is a lot of smoke, but then the blaze gets going, flares up above the rim of the barrel. Both of us stare into the fire. Soon we will look up and be surprised at how dark it has become, how long we have been standing there.

"I have something to tell you," my father says. He tells me this story.

He went away to college on an early September evening in 1948. A couple of hours before sunset, he left for St. John's, planning to stay there overnight and, in the morning, catch the train for Port aux Basques. It would be his first crossing of the island and his first crossing of the Gulf, his first time off the island. He was twenty-three years old. The age that I am now.

He said all but one of his goodbyes in the house. His father, on some pretext, had gone down to the beach. My father, leaving his suitcases by the car of a family friend who was waiting to drive him to St. John's, walked down to the beach where Charlie was standing, looking out across the water.

Charlie did not want my father to leave. He was crying when my father reached him on the beach. They hugged but said nothing. My father made his way back up the beach, sliding in his best shoes on the rocks. His father, who had continued to face the water, turned when he stopped hearing the clatter of rocks behind him, when my father reached the grassy slope that led up to the road.

"Be a good boy!" his father shouted. My twenty-three-year-old father turned and looked at Charlie standing there a few feet from the water, not quite turned to face him, one arm lifted and dropped quickly in a gesture of resigned farewell.

Then Charlie fully faced the sea again, put his hands on his hips, looked out across the Pool, between Bois Island and Ferryland Head, at the open water. He stood there in that reflective, stock-taking pose, facing the direction exactly opposite the one his son would soon be taking.

So he left in defiance of his father. But surely something more must have happened on that beach. I look at my father as he stares into the fire. Before I can ask him to, he tells me more.

He went away to college in September of 1948, crossing an island that was still a country but whose days as such were numbered. While he was away, Newfoundland the country ceased to be. At college in Truro, Nova Scotia, on April 1, 1949, induction day, the day Newfoundland joined Confederation, my father was set upon by a group of his mainland friends who hoisted him on their shoulders and, ignoring his protests that he would always be a Newfoundlander and the fact that tears were streaming down his face, carried him around the campus shouting, "Three cheers for the new Canadian!"

He pauses again. There is no way I will let him tell me this much and not tell me the rest. "I skipped a bit," he says.

Something else happened while he was away at college, a few months before Confederation.

His father died. I never knew this until now, had never taken notice of the date of Charlie's death when looking at his headstone on the Gaze.

Charlie died about halfway through the nine-month interval between the second referendum and induction day. Despite losing the referendum, he had died a Newfoundlander, in

January of 1949. The two referenda in the summer of 1948, the two nights six weeks apart that he spent crouched beside the radio, arms around his stomach, rocking slowly back and forth as if silently trying to coax the anti-confederates to victory as the results were coming in, the excruciating closeness of the votes, the campaign between the inconclusive referendum and the next, then the months of waiting after their defeat for induction day — all this had proved too much for him.

He had fretted himself to death as the countdown to Confederation proceeded, each day changing on a schoolroom slate that he hung on the wall in the kitchen the number of days left in the life of Newfoundland. Charlie died on January 14, 1949, the day after erasing the number 77 and hours after writing the number 76 on the slate.

Throughout the three days of his wake and funeral, the slate, like a stopped clock, read 76. Afterwards, Nan could neither stand the sight of it, reminder, register that it was of the day he died, nor bring herself to erase the number, so she took the slate down and put it out of sight and out of mind on a table in the attic. She took the top of a tin biscuit box and with the box turned upside down enclosed the number-bearing slate and left it there. That she did this was not discovered until some years later, when Nan herself died and Eva, plundering the house for keepsakes, found the slate where her mother had left it; not knowing there was anything beneath it, she picked up the biscuit box, disinterring the slate, which still faintly bore, in her father's hand, the number of days Newfoundland had outlived him.

Poor Eva almost fainted. "I think she still has the slate," my father said. "But I don't know if you can read the number any more."

When my father and Charlie parted on the beach, they knew that by the time they met again, something dear to both of them would have ceased to be, and that this would happen while they were hundreds of miles apart. But they did not meet again.

It was not because he was embarrassed to have his family see him cry that Charlie left the house and went down to the beach. He went there because he and my father had had a falling-out about something.

My father pauses in the story he is telling. There are no lights on in the house, which makes me think my mother might be watching.

"This falling-out. It was about you not wanting to be a fisherman?" I say.

My father smiles, shakes his head. "No," he says. "It was nothing. Just some little thing. I don't even remember what it was."

It is so dark now that if not for the fire, I would not be able to see his face. There is no way he could tell me this without us having the fire to look at while he speaks. "You must remember what it was," I say.

"I don't," he says. "I really don't."

I know he remembers and I try to think it through. It was to Canada that my father was going, to Canada at this of all times, the country he esteemed no more highly than Charlie did, but he had no choice, there being no college at that time in Newfoundland. To Canada, which Newfoundland would become part of while he was away. It must have seemed to Charlie like a betrayal. And when his father died while he was in Canada, how must my father have felt? Somehow to blame perhaps. Against all assurances to the contrary — and there must have been many — somehow to blame.

For my father, as for all the Johnstons, it was not "immediately before the expiration of March 31, 1949," as set out in the Terms of Union, but with Charlie's passing that the old Newfoundland ceased to be. His death divided the century and, more effectively than anything else the chronophobic Charlie could have done, kept his children rooted in both time and space, imposed on them an obligation to continue, however pointlessly or tokenly, to resist Confederation. Confederation and the death of their father were forever twinned in their minds.

I think now that I have the whole story, a complete explanation why my father almost never talks about his father, and why my aunts and uncles never do, and why there are no photographs of Charlie in the house.

But there is more.

From Truro to Ferryland is not far, was not far, even then. But he had no money and neither did his family. All of them together could not scrape up the train fare to bring him home to see his father waked and buried. The cost of Charlie's funeral left them penniless.

He stayed in his residence room at college, his door locked for three days, while five hundred miles away, across the Gulf, his father was being waked and buried, and he alone of all the Johnstons was not there. At last some of his friends climbed in through his window and dragged him outdoors.

"Be a good boy," Charlie Johnston said to my father on the beach at Ferryland. A begrudging blessing. Good boy. Not quite a goodbye. Good boy.

I try to imagine them on the beach at Ferryland.

It is little more than a month since the referendum. Every emotion is heightened. The whole of Ferryland, the whole of Newfoundland, is nervously exhausted. Hard on the heels of losing the referendum, Charlie is losing his son. Another casting-off. It is early September. As usual, the seasons have a month's jump on the calendar. The low scrub on the Downs has begun to turn, the smell of fall has been in the air for weeks. A winter is coming that will be my father's first away from home, a succession of December days when darkness will fall between four and five o'clock.

The last thing they share is that prospect from the beach. The only thing they see that a person on the same spot looking seaward five hundred years ago would not have seen is the lighthouse on the Head. Nothing else has been added or subtracted except by nature, incrementally, imperceptibly. "Be a good boy," Charlie says. And my father, thus admonished, leaves his father standing there.

It is 1981, thirty-two years since Confederation, thirty-three since Charlie died. My father will not ask me not to leave, or plead with me not to or come as close as Charlie did to begrudging his son what might be a last goodbye. There is no reason to think that we will not meet again. He is only fifty-three, not as old as Charlie, who died years before his time at fifty-six. But I know he will not take the chance. He knows how it would be for me and for him if we parted on bad or ambiguous terms or even awkwardly.

Each of us has a stick to poke at the cardboard. Embers float up from the barrel, go out, become flankers of grey ash above our heads and drift slowly pondward, carried by a breeze so faint that we cannot feel it. I look up at the ridge, the crest of which marks the start of what we think of as the woods because you cannot hike there and back unless you spend a night outdoors. I have done it many times, gone down into the valley on the other side and slept on the ground.

I wonder if I have lived in this house long enough, have looked out on this prospect often enough for it to be imprinted on my brain as the view from the house on the Gaze is on his, if years from now, when I speak about Forest Pond, the Shoal Bay Hills, the Petty Harbour Road, I will call them the Pond, the Hills, the Road. I doubt it. For though I have not yet seen much of the world, I know that I am going to, and though I have not yet travelled even as far from Newfoundland as he has, I will have done so and then some by this time tomorrow night.

The Gaze, the Pool, Hare's Ears. I will dwell more on his landmarks than I will on mine. This is what I think when I am twenty-three. Perhaps he thought like that when he stood with Charlie on the beach; perhaps he thought the place he was soon to leave had more of a hold on his father than it did on him.

As I stare into the fire, it reminds me of the forge, which in my lifetime was never lit. I almost say so, then think better of it.

"We'll throw your stuff in now," my father says. The cardboard has burnt. We start throwing in the contents of the box.

"So you're off to college tomorrow, Wayne," my father says. I wondered when he would get round to it.

"Yeah," I say with a brisk enthusiasm I hope will discourage him from getting sentimental.

"I wish I was you," he said. "I'd love to be your age again."

"Yeah," I say, but this time in a different tone, for I think I know exactly how he feels. I say it with a wistful sympathy, as if I myself have often wished that I was younger. But it is not just younger that he wants to be, of course. He wants to be back there, on the other side of the moment when he turned and left his father on the beach. But also he wants me to understand, now, how great a thing it is to be my age, to revel in the sense of possibility and the knowledge of how much of my life still lies before me. No twenty-three-year-old has ever understood such things, but he wants me to. And he wants to dispel any sadness or apprehension I may have about leaving. He has just conferred on me his blessing. What greater blessing could he give to what I was doing than to wish that he were me? It does not undo or make up for Charlie's admonition, his last words to his twenty-three-year-old son, "Be a good boy." But he has overcome, at least long enough to spare me its effects, a sorrow that might have made such tenderness impossible.

We throw more pages in, ripping pages out of notebooks, tearing them in half. It is like some arch symbolic gesture, a purging of my past.

I look up and already I can see some stars. I can dimly see the ridge against the sky. I can smell the grass where a sheen of dew has begun to form and, from the stand of alders just outside the fence, the first faint rot of fall.

A thought, a doubt that will nag at me for years, occurs to me. He was young. Not much older than I am now. There is more to the story, there is, palpably, something more. Did he blurt out something to Charlie on the beach before he left, to Charlie who was so ashamed that he never told another soul? There is more. I am sure of it. Does he want me to say so, ask him what else there is, as if I am hearing his confession? Surely he wouldn't, having told this much, not tell the rest.

This cannot be *it*, I feel like saying. There is something here that no one knows but you. Perhaps he wants me to say that, wants me to coax him into giving this story the ending it deserves, an ending that would make sense to me. "Be a good boy," I half expect he would say if I asked him to swear that he has told me everything he knows.

Now it occurs to me what he might be holding back.

But of course I cannot ask him. Not being sure that I am right, I cannot ask him *that*. If I do and I am wrong, we will part the way that he and Charlie did. There is even more symmetry here than I imagined. The only way I can find out why they parted on bad terms is by risking parting on bad terms with him. If my suspicions are right, he must know that I can never ask him to confirm them. Unless he offers, I may never know.

I look at him and remember the night we came back on the train from Port aux Basques. His whispered conversation with his brother the night he fled the party and went outdoors. I remember the change that came over him whenever we came in sight of Ferryland and the day he did not come back down with the others when they went up to the Gaze to see his parents' graves. I remember all the times I heard him speak of that "something" that happened on the beach.

"I'm sure going to miss this place," I say.

He nods. "I already do and I'm still here. Who knows? You might come back. I did."

Again I am grateful for the fire, this third presence, to our tending of which talk is incidental. We stay at the barrel until the blaze dies down. I can feel the heat of it receding from my face. Now the sky is banked with stars. Above the Shoal Bay Hills, the moon is rising, nearly full, so close to the horizon that it looks twice its size.

"There'll be a ring around the moon tonight," my father says.

And he is right. Later, looking out my window, I see the storm-portending ring. If this were winter, a real beauty of a blizzard would be on its way, the kind that in my childhood kept me spellbound at the windows, which afterwards always bore the marks of my ten fingers and my nose.

But it is fall and rain is coming, a storm that now is in the Gulf and getting stronger. By noon tomorrow it will have sent ahead of it like fair warning a front of cloud and a gale of wind. And on this place that from this window I will never see again the rain will fall.

HE STANDS ON the beach, looking out across the Pool. He knows his son is watching from the kitchen window. They have put off their goodbye as long as possible. He is waiting for him.

His son will keep his secret. There are many who would, but only if he asked them to. He will not have to ask his son.

But he must not try to justify himself or seem to be looking for consolation or forgiveness. All he wants is to rid himself of the loneliness he has felt these past two months. The priest told him once that "in confession you confess, but elsewhere you confide."

He is waiting for him to come down to the beach. He will simply tell him and it will be *their* secret. He wishes he had told him sooner. They might be over it by now. If he was able to imagine what his son would say or do, he would prepare himself. How long will it take? As long as to walk from the window to the door?

His son will soon be far away. He could write to him or wait until he comes back home from college in the spring. But he feels that if he does not tell him now he never will.

Every day, long before last light, the shadow of the Gaze falls on the Pool. You only notice that the water has changed colour. You never see it change.

Not even as he hears the front door open and then close does he know what his first word will be. He thinks: in a moment he will know and the world will come between us.

At the sound of footsteps on the rocks, he drops his hands from his hips and turns around.

The first word that he speaks is Arthur's name.

I LEFT BY boat, as I had vowed I would when I first saw the Gulf when I was ten. The sight of Newfoundland slowly receding reminded me of something. I could not think what until we were several miles offshore. It was not what I had anticipated I would think about as I was leaving. I'd imagined a Stephen Dedalus–like sense of expectation and adventure, standing like Joyce's hero at the rail, open-armed for new lands and new experience, casting off the nets that for so long had held me back. Instead, it was the "resettlers" I thought about.

This was how the island must have looked to those Newfoundlanders whom the government resettled from remote islands to population centres in the sixties. This must have been what they had seen when they looked out their windows, this horizon-obscuring chunk of rock on which they had never set foot and vowed they never would.

It was not what most of them had seen while they made the final crossing to the "mainland," for they sailed away with their eyes on their islands and their backs to Newfoundland and did not turn around until they disembarked. Most of them had to be coaxed from boats that in some cases had been moored for hours to wharves and fishing stages. I would probably have done the same thing if it was possible to see Newfoundland from the ferry all the way to Nova Scotia.

A great-uncle of mine who was born in Ferryland at some point visited Woody Island, got married there and never left it until the people of Woody Island were resettled in 1968 to Arnold's Cove. We went out to Arnold's Cove to see him and his family land like immigrants on the shore of Newfoundland and to see their house floated across the bay on a raft buoyed up by oil drums.

We were not the only ones there. It was a summer week-end pastime for people to drive out around the bay and see houses floated in from the offshore islands. There were a couple of dozen people, some with binoculars, staring out to sea as if waiting for some annual event of nature. Woody Island was too far away to differentiate one house from another. There were merely clumps of colours near the shore. I saw a wedge of green detach itself like an iceberg from a glacier, then a great eruption of white water. "Whoa," a man looking through binoculars said. We would not have been surprised had we been told the house had sunk, but soon we saw the green again.

While my parents and my aunts and uncles went down to the wharf to welcome my all-but-mythical great-uncle and his never-before-glimpsed relatives, my brothers and I climbed the hill to get a better view of the houses as they came, towed by tugs and motorboats, across the bay. The houses tilted forward slightly in spite of the oil drums. The front of the rafts dipped below the water, and waves lapped at the windowless storm doors, the houses plowing a wide slow wake, pushing rounded swells in front of them, a small fleet of square-hulled ships. I expected to see people inside them, leaning out the windows, expected the front doors to open and people to peer out to see how close to shore they were. But the houses were just shells. You could see right through them, the sunlit empty rooms, bare walls.

The owners escorted their houses in skiffs piled high with everything they owned, loads of precariously balanced furniture, cardboard boxes of belongings, the skiffs riding so low that their gunwales barely cleared the water, their engines putt-putting just fast enough to keep from stalling.

I had heard that in mid-crossing some houses, made top-heavy by their chimneys and their roofs, caved in, or, the upper storeys tilting too far forward, broke in half. My great-uncle's house made it to Arnold's Cove without mishap and was winched up a slipway to a flatbed truck.

But one woman, one of his sisters-in-law I think it was, refused to get out of the boat when it moored at the wharf. Wearing a nylon scarf tightly tied beneath her chin, a bulky overcoat, lime green slacks and a pair of rubber kneeboots, she sat staring out across the bay. People on the wharf tried to coax her out of the boat, but, her back to Arnold's Cove, her eyes on Woody Island, she shook her head. Finally two men climbed down into the boat and she let herself be led to the ladder. When she stepped onto the wharf, she covered her face with her hands, shaking her head when two women put their arms around her, as if she would not be consoled.

I wondered how long I would last in the place where I was headed if from there I could still see Newfoundland, and knew that I could not go back, not ever. I thought of the stories my father had told me, the moral of which, until now, I had taken to be that outporters were hopelessly set in their ways, hopelessly old-fashioned and opposed to change.

When he was travelling the south coast on the *Belle Bay*, he saw houses being moved. Each house was blessed by a priest or a minister before being launched. The priest walked about the empty rooms and sprinkled holy water with a sceptre that he dipped from time to time in a little silver bucket. Fighting water with water. It was hoped that these drops that spattered on the floors and on the walls and on the windows would keep out the sea.

The houses, and the rafts to which they were bound, went down the slips like boats being launched. A great cheer rose when, after the suspense of the initial plunge and the bobbing up and down, a house floated upright and the swell that might have swamped it subsided. A seaworthy house.

The closest thing to a crowd that you could get in places that size gathered for each launching. The whole thing seemed to my father foredoomed by the desire of these people to take their houses with them when they could have opted to have a new house built free of charge on a site of their own choosing. They would rather risk sinking it than leave it behind. So how then would they live without what they could not help but leave behind — the view they had had all their lives from its windows? Opening the same door as they had before they moved, looking out the same window, they would never stop expecting to see what they used to see outside.

The resettlers took with them their flagpoles and their painted beach rocks, their clothesline posts and barrels for burning trash. They took with them, so they could litter their new yards with them, objects that had lain about their old yards for decades, punctured buoys, laddered fishing nets and broken lobster traps.

Many people moved to places from which they could see their old homes a few miles of water away. This did not relieve their homesickness, of course, but only made it worse. It was difficult even for the men who had often seen their island from a distance, seen it resolve into shapes and lines as they looked back at it while they were heading out to sea, seen it as, from their boats that lay anchored, they handlined for cod. They looked up and there it was, *their* island. But for many of the women who had never or only rarely been off their island in their lives, the sudden shift in perspective was too profound. They might as well have been marooned astronauts looking back at the moon from planet Earth.

My father told me that a church while being relocated sprang a leak and sank and still lay at the bottom of the sea, and that its bell could still be heard, a muffled submarine sound that went faintly out across the bay when the tides were running or when the sea was rough.

He said that houses sinking were cut loose to keep them from dragging under the boats that were towing them. Some, set adrift but only half submerged, floated out to sea where, looming suddenly out of the fog as if they had been wrenched by tidal waves from their foundations, they scared the life out of fishermen, nudging against their boats and then moving on as if they were being navigated from below the waterline by someone looking out the kitchen window.

There flashed through my mind the image of our bungalow on Petty Harbour Road attached by a tow line to the ferry, my parents at the windows smiling and waving at me. It seemed so absurd I almost laughed out loud.

Knowing I would lose sight of Newfoundland eventually, I did not stand at the rail. Instead I sat facing away from it for as long as I was able to resist the urge to look. And when finally I did look, it was gone.

THE CABIN WAS built by someone who had either changed his mind about being a hermit or had gone to be one somewhere else. Now it was being rented by some Newfoundlander who had talked himself into believing it was a sure bet, the first of many cabins he would buy or build on abandoned islands and rent to mainlanders who had run out of places to go to get away. This much I had found out from the fellow who took me out to the island in the boat he used to fish from before the fish ran out. I had told him I was from St. John's, but I might as well have said Los Angeles, for he seemed to draw no distinction between one place he had never been to and another.

The cabin looks like something you would see at the entrance to a park for Sunday hikers, made from what might be imitation logs they are so lacquered, so polished. I can tell I will not be roughing it until I go outdoors, which is fine with me. Having been away from Newfoundland for five years, I came back three years ago and now, at the age of thirty, am trying to decide if I should leave again, knowing that if I do it will be for good. No amount of weighing the pros and cons inclines me one way or the other. I have come to realize that in this choice, reason must have no say.

My hope is that, here, nudged by some solitary impulse, my mind will somehow make itself up, sparing me the task. Everywhere I've been there are people I can live among, or stand to live among, as it sometimes seems. I have to know if I can live without the land. Perhaps out here, where there is nothing but the land, I can decide. I have prescribed myself a week of solitude, a week without once dwelling on the question or otherwise considering my destiny or that of anyone I know. I can therefore read as much as I like but I am not allowed to write.

For electricity, there is a small generator. There is no running water, but there is a room brim-full of light-blue coolers stacked like wine casks at the back. There is no phone, but there is a short-wave radio rigged so that all I have to do in case of trouble is flip a switch and ask for help.

The place is well stocked with food and wood. There is a new wood stove that has a window at the front so it doubles as a fireplace. In the bedroom there is a real fireplace with bricks so pristine it must never have been used.

In case the tenant has not come properly prepared, there is winter clothing that would do for climbing mountains, as well as snow goggles and snowshoes that snap on like skis.

On the inside of the front door are instructions about what you should and should not do when you leave the cabin. Once you open the door on arrival, don't use the key again until you leave. NEVER LOCK THE DOOR. No matter how hard the snow is near the cabin, never leave without your snowshoes.

On the adjoining wall, a poster offers a crash course in winter weather. The freezing point of water. A formula for calculating wind chill. Using your thermometer. Using your barometer. DON'T BE FOOLED: LOW PRESSURE MEANS BAD WEATHER. An admonishment to stay indoors, no matter how nice it appears to be outside, if the air pressure drops two readings in a row. It all seems overdone, designed to impress on city dwellers just how wild this wilderness adventure is. Radio forecasts are helpful, but local conditions can vary widely within the forecast zone. A chart shows how long you can safely stay outdoors at certain sub-zero temperatures. Of little use to me because I have no watch. Any watch I wear or even put in my pocket keeps time unreliably and within a week or so stops altogether. I have been told by jewellers that for some unknown reason, a small number of people have this effect on watches.

I have never spent much time in winter this close to the sea. No one need ever have told me how long a man who went overboard into *that* would last. I can tell just from looking at it. How can anything warm-blooded have had its origins in that? No blizzard, no iceberg, no howling northwest wind is cold the way that water is. On the crest sides, the waves are rippled by the wind, on the trough sides as smooth and black as slate. Not snow or ice or wind, or any feature of geography present to the inhabitant or traveller the kind of obstacle this water does. Any place between you and which there is land is more real than a place from which you are separated by the sea.

An island to someone who has never left it *is* the world. An island to someone who has never seen it does not exist.

At night I try not to dwell on my isolation, partly out of

a fear for my safety that by day I do not feel. Any help summoned by short-wave to this place might be days in coming. I
read constantly for companionship, to get back into the world.
If this island had never been inhabited, if evidence that, at one
time, the place was lived in was not scattered everywhere, I
would feel less lonely.

I do not realize until I see the beaver house that I am halfway
across a pond. Straight ahead, just visible above the snow, is a
beaver dam and in front of it a triangle of slush ending in a
stretch of open water. I turn around and gingerly retrace my
steps, knowing that if I were not wearing snowshoes I would
already have gone through the ice. I am lucky that the snow is
deep. I guess that nothing smaller than a stunted spruce has seen
the light of day since last November. It is the snow, more than
the ice, that holds me up. The ice, insulated by the snow, is
probably only about two inches thick. I am almost at the shore
when the snow and ice give way beneath me. I go in up to my
waist and then hit bottom, fall for a suspenseful fraction of a
second until I stop in mud that, because of the snowshoes, I
don't sink into very far. Feeling foolish, I pull myself out without much difficulty and crawl on my stomach the last few feet
to shore. By the time I reach the cabin, my snow pants are as
stiff as cardboard and the snowshoes so encrusted with frozen
mud that I can barely lift my feet.

I have just had the sort of mishap on which the sort of
person for whom this cabin was designed would dine out for
years. A brush with death in the wilderness by which his city-
weary spirit was renewed. It was also the sort of mishap that
could have been much worse, that could have left me just as

dead as that greenhorn from the mainland. I had walked, like some out-of-his-element thrill seeker, across what, when I was twelve, I would have known was a barely frozen mudhole.

Now the warning on the door seems like a compilation of advice from tenants who learned the hard way what the hazards are. I add to the list, writing on a piece of paper that I tack to the wall: "Be careful where you walk. When the snow is deep, there is no telling where the land leaves off and the ponds begin. Remember that every step you take might be your last. Perils abound and woe to him who, having read my warning, heeds it not. 'Doom is dark and deeper than any sea-dingle.'" Let my successor try to figure that one out.

For the first two days I avoid the abandoned settlement that is the main attraction for the tourists who come here in the summertime. I tell myself I have no intention of mooning homiletically about in some ghost town. But I find it impossible, knowing that it's there, not to take a look. The hermit built just out of sight of the settlement, just around the shore from it, as if to have built within sight of it would have been too intrusive, would somehow have spoiled the place.

Most of the houses that are left are shells of wood. There is one structure that might have been a school. The various parts of it seem not to touch. It seems to be held up by the space that it encloses. Everything has been taken from here, every detachable, man-made, non-wooden thing. Glass, chimney pots, stoves, pails, anchors.

There is a church from which the stained glass windows have been carefully removed, even the porthole-like window in the steeple on top of which a rusting crucifix still stands. It is like some sort of reduced-scale, model church, six rows of pews on either side, a narrow aisle between them leading to the altar. Between the windows are small wooden shelves still bearing the rings of the oil lamps that once rested on them. Trails of soot climb the walls above the shelves, and there are faint soot circles on the ceiling. The floor, the pews, the stripped-bare altar are strewn with leaves, twigs, orange needles from the blasty boughs of spruce trees. The side of the church that for the better part of the day is in the shade is damp and grown over with green mould and moss. In the cabin there is no brochure explaining who these people were, when and why they settled here and when they left.

In front of the church is a small cemetery. I have to dig away the snow from the headstones to read their inscriptions. There are eleven thin, semicircular white marble stones with black inscriptions, all of which bear the same last name, as if no marriages or births took place here, as if some family, after generations of attrition, died out. Some member of the family must have led the service every Sunday. They came here in pursuit of an absolute of self-sufficiency, a family resigned or even dedicated to its own extinction. Some of the men and women might have met and married people from elsewhere and left the island, though it is hard to imagine how these meetings would have taken place. They built on the eastern side of the island, the side that faced away from Newfoundland. From here no other islands can be seen, just the sea whose storms they took the brunt of rather than live on the leeward, land-facing side. It might have been a gesture of renunciation. Or perhaps it was just that here they were closer to the fishing grounds.

There is a feeling different from what you get in landlocked ghost towns, the sense of a whole world, a whole history having ended. It is like some elaborately, painstakingly constructed object lesson, the kind of place that might have made the author of Ecclesiastes feel that the writing of his book was a foolish act of vanity and a striving after wind.

It is impossible not to feel the ghostly past of the place. At night, in the distance, I see the lights of passing ships. When it is time to take the lantern from the window, time to turn the wick down low and make my way through my unfamiliar house and go to bed, I try to imagine what my light must look like to someone watching from out there. Seeing it fade until nothing is left but a spark so faint they must wonder if it is real — and then know it is, for abruptly it is gone. Nothing now. No prospect but the dark.

This barometer, like the ones of my childhood, measures pressure in degrees instead of in kilopascals. On my third day, it registers the largest one-tap drop I have ever seen, three full points from thirty-two to twenty-nine. I have never even heard of pressure dropping under twenty-nine except at the sudden onset of tornadoes or hurricanes. My father often told me that the worst wind that ever blew across the island was nothing next to the worst wind that ever blew ten miles from shore, let alone two hundred.

A storm, a great storm, is coming. I feel as though there is no point in my being here if I stay inside. There a hill directly behind the cabin, without ever straying from the lee of which you can reach the church. In defiance of the instructions on the door, I put on my snowshoes and go up to the church to wait for the storm to start.

There used to be full-length shutters on the north-facing windows that when open folded outward and were bolted to the wall. They have left arch-shaped shadows in the clapboard. There were no shutters on the south side of the church, which is so much in the lee of the hill I doubt the ground beneath the windows ever sees the sun.

At first I stand at the middle of the three windows, the wind hitting me full in the face. The snow does not begin with flurries. It comes in across the water like an accelerated bank of fog and forces me back as it pelts in slant-wise, flecked with ice that stings my face. I have to move farther and farther back to avoid it, standing sideways between the pews, then in the aisle, then in the other row of pews. The storm is only minutes under way when the drifting starts. The snow spouts through the windows like water held back for ages and at last released, three torrents of it gushing in.

I stand just out of range of the snow. I reach out my hand as though into the mist on the far fringe of a waterfall, then draw my hand back, cold and dripping wet. The snow is deepest on the floor beneath the window. From there it slopes off slowly until, about two-thirds of the way across to the leeward side, it peters out just inches from my feet. It adheres to the walls between the windows, to the pews. Eventually the snow will back me up against the wall and I will have to leave. I wonder if it is possible that the wind will blow so hard that the snow will come in through one window and go out the corresponding one on the other side.

It is as though the windows are hung with large white drapes that, when the wind is at its height, are almost horizontal to the floor, then flutter downward as the wind subsides.

I have never heard a sound like the wind makes as it funnels through the windows, a shrieking whistle whose upper pitch seems to have no limit. I can only hear the sifting snow between the gusts, hear it on the floor of the church and on the ground outside, snow on snow, the island's terrain shape-shifting by the minute.

The greatest gusts of wind slam the whole wall at once. If not for the open windows that disperse the force, I think the wall and the whole church with it would give way. Ships larger than this island have gone down in lesser storms. Yet I feel certain that having withstood so many storms, the church will hold up through this one. I know that I can make it to the cabin in half an hour as long as I set out before the sun goes down.

Almost no snow comes in through the windows on the leeward side. If not for them, the church, with each gust of wind, would go completely dark, for the whiteout is so dense that no light comes through.

They lived here, those people buried in that little cemetery. When a storm like this came up, they could not tell themselves that soon they would be living somewhere else. For them there was no last straw. Alternatives were so unheard of they did not know they had none.

A seagull glides down from the choir loft, banks slowly, goes out the nearest leeward window, returns a moment later through the middle one, rising, still gliding until he clears the balustrade. Behind it, with a fluttering of wings that I can hear but cannot see, he lands. A show of grace, a show of force. There must be a nest up there, I think, until I remember that no bird would nest this early in the year.

He repeats the performance, rises up on a fluttering of wings, glides down from the loft, out one window, in the other and goes back to the loft again.

He thinks that like him, I have taken refuge here and lack the sense to join him in the loft, where it must be warmer and where there is no snow, which he wants me to do, not out of any concern for my welfare but because he knows that sooner or later I will discover the loft. He is telling me, before I try to chase him off, that he is willing to share it.

I have no intention of spending the night in here, but I accept his invitation. Removing my snowshoes, I test the steps that lead up to the loft to see if they will hold my weight, which they do, though the boards creak loudly. It is ten steps or so to the loft, where there is a single pew with space enough for four or five people, half the congregation if the cemetery is anything to go by. Perhaps when the church was built the family had hopes of being joined by others who never came.

The seagull roosts on the other side of the loft, hard to the wall, eyeing me with some nervousness at first. I was right. There is no nest. As a nesting place, it is too obvious and too accessible.

I stand at the balustrade and look out across the church as the triple torrents blast in through the windows. I feel as though I am looking down from the as yet unflooded floor of some sinking ship. It *is* much warmer up here, not as drafty as I expected it would be, dry and sheltered from the winds that eddy about inside the church. I sit down, my back against the wall, as far from the gull as I can get.

The weariness that comes over you when you warm up after a long time in the cold makes me nod off. Waking, I think for a panicked moment that I have slept past sunset, but actually it has been only minutes, for the church, when I stand up, looks just the same. Still, I tell myself, I might never have woken up, or might have woken freezing in the middle of the night.

I go down the stairs with a haste that startles the gull. After I snap on my snowshoes, I climb out one of the lee windows. Looking back, I see the gull soar among the rafters of the old white church, out of the reach of the snow that swirls below him, out of mine.

Tonight, on hundreds of such islands around the coast of Newfoundland, in restored houses, in cottages and cabins much more primitive than mine, others wait out the storm, which they know may last for days. It is partly for such intervals of enforced idleness and confinement that they have chosen to winter here. Snow blots out the world by day as well as the darkness does by night. And day and night there will be no sound outside but that of the wind that blows from where the melting of the old ice stalled ten thousand years ago.

Nothing on the radio but shrieks of static that seem to be mimicking the storm. I remember my proscription not to dwell on my destiny or that of anyone I know, not to write, but tonight I cannot help it.

There are roads you can travel to where they were abandoned fifty years ago, to piers at which boats from smaller islands docked when their owners made the trip to Newfoundland. On each of these islands there is a hermitage where at night a lone light burns. In them live people who will never double back, for whom history has been suspended and nationality is obsolete. Some of them are people who, instead of leaving with the fleets of floating houses in the sixties, stayed behind. Others, from the main island of Newfoundland or even from the continent, went back to these abandoned islands whose populations in the census thereby rose from none to one or two.

They can see from where they live the life that they declined, or the lights of that life anyway, the lights of towns and especially on cloudy nights the glow from cities in the sky. They see lines of lights that trace out the shapes of roads they have never used or whose use they have forsworn. Like their fellows on the main island, they are the hard-core holdouts. They keep vigil for a destiny that will never be resumed, commemorate a life they know is lost. I am not one of them. I cannot hold that vigil with them.

But I am still drawn down those dead-end roads at night to the sea and the piers from which the lantern lights in houses on islands far from shore can still be seen. I told my father once when I was too young to have sense enough to keep the observation to myself that as these islands were to Newfoundland, so Newfoundland was to the world. He smiled and said nothing. He did not want to be fated to irresolution, or a life of protest, did not want to be a man without a country or a patriot of one that never was. But neither could he pledge an allegiance that he did not feel. "The land," he once told me, "is more important than the country. The land is there before you when you close your eyes at night and still there in the morning when you wake. No one can make off with the land the way they made off with the country in 1949."

He told me the story of the Newfoundlanders travelling abroad with passports deemed by our new government to be good until 1954. For years after Confederation, they travelled the world as Newfoundlanders, itinerant citizens of a country that, since they saw it last, had ceased to be. In no sense were these people anything but Newfoundlanders until the first time they set foot on "native" soul, or until their five years were up. There were supposed to be some who neither came back home nor acquired new passports from the Canadian embassies in their countries of residence. Instead, they stayed away in protest, in self-exile from the country that now occupied their own. I loved the idea of these Newfoundlanders in the States, in England, Germany or France blending in among foreigners, still carrying their outdated passports. Citizens of no country, staging their futile, furtive, solitary protests that were at once so grand and so absurd. I wasn't even sure if there were such people, or if it was possible for anyone to live that way for long without detection. But it was a good story. And for someone who, like me, was born after 1949, the very existence of the country known as Newfoundland was just a story, composed of countless stories I had been told or read in books, of exhibits in museums, of monuments and statues and inscription-bearing plaques.

The country of no country is a story almost as enduring as the land.

IN 1992, NOT long after the cod fishery was closed, my parents phoned and told me they were leaving Newfoundland, going to Alberta, where my brothers and their children lived.

"The Newfoundland I knew is gone," my father said.

He said it regretfully, but it also sounded a little like wishful thinking — wishful thinking that it might not be too late to escape the pull of the past. He was hoping that space would do what time had not. I considered telling him so but decided not to. The house was sold. The arrangements were already made and their minds made up.

Was it possible that three thousand miles from home, in the heart of the continent, morning would not find him brooding at the window, that a day might pass when he did not think of Charlie and the moment of their parting on the beach, that not every day would feel as though the referendum had been newly lost or feel like induction day? It might not be too late for him, for them to not mind that nationality was obsolete, that it no longer mattered where they lived because the Newfoundland they loved, *their* Newfoundland, did not exist.

He had been in the college lab in January of 1949 examining soil samples under a microscope, lost in this just-discovered other world, when one of his professors called him out into the hall and handed him a telegram from his brother Gordon that ended with the words "Come home." Was it possible, three thousand miles from home, that he would think of that less often?

It must have *seemed* possible. It must have seemed, in those days before they left, that anything was possible. And it must not often seem so when you are in your sixties. Moving might be worth it, just for that.

It was only when my parents left it that I really felt that I had left Newfoundland. I had been living away from Newfoundland for most of the past twelve years, in Toronto for the last three.

It seemed for a while that my past had been erased, that my memory extended back no further than my twenties, as if I had had amnesia since then and knew only where my last twelve years were spent. And even when this feeling passed, my memories of home seemed less legitimate, almost counterfeit, the importance I had invested them with foolishly overblown, as if they could not have been worth much, having happened in a place that everyone I loved had left. Like me, all my brothers and sisters had left. But it had felt as if I had remained true to home, could not be said to have abandoned it, as long as my parents were there.

Their decision to leave came from out of the blue, as their decisions to move house when I was a child had. I remembered coming home from school one day to find my grandfather's truck in the yard, piled high with all our furniture. We were moving again, but I had not known it until that moment when I saw the truck. I had not known when I left the house that morning that I would never set foot inside of it again. That was exactly how I felt when they told me on the phone that they were selling the house. I had not known when I last left it that I would never see the inside of it again.

The thought of them by themselves in a house in a place as unlike Newfoundland as the Prairies filled me with such dread that for nights I could not sleep. I was anxious, for them, I thought. What would happen to them? How could they possibly, at their ages, manage such a move?

It was a long time before I realized that they might not miss it as much as I would miss their being there.

During his last days in Newfoundland, he listened to the *Fishermen's Broadcast* on the CBC, the one I used to listen to as a child when he was off on a tour of the south coast, the broadcast that, out of habit, the idle fishermen still listened to as gale and freezing-spray warnings were issued for stretches of water where no fishing boats had sailed for years.

He listened to the "temperature roundup," which gave the present temperature and weather conditions in places around the island, the places they used to visit in the *Belle Bay* or landed offshore from in a seaplane and walked to across the ice, places he hadn't seen in years but each of which he pictured when the announcer said its name, isolated, desolate places he was glad he no longer had to go to, yet somehow missed or thought he did. Perhaps the names just reminded him of time if not quite wasted then inscrutably disappointing, time that should have yielded something more, for him, for Newfoundland, though what that something was he couldn't say.

There were many last things that had to be done. They had to bid goodbye to mystified relatives and friends who could not help feeling abandoned and betrayed. There was no time to give everyone more of an explanation than this: they were leaving to be with their children, going to the province where those of their children who had children lived. This was not the real reason and they knew it, but they did not know what the real reason was. A last trip had to be made to Ferryland to see Gordon and Rita, Millie, Kitty. My father had to climb the Gaze and say goodbye to Nan and Charlie.

On the Downs, the archaeologists who were still looking for the ruins of Baltimore's mansion had uncovered the ashes of a nearly four-hundred-year-old forge. The first blacksmith's forge in the New World. The forge that Wynne had written about from Ferryland to Lord Baltimore in England: "The Forge hath been finished this five weeks."

A last trip had to be made to old St. John's to see Eva in her hillside house that overlooked the harbour. Eva tried to talk them out of leaving and, failing, consoled herself by predicting they would soon come back. Something they thought was permanent but that was really only temporary had come over them, she said, though she did not say what that something was.

Though they were in their sixties, the time had come, as it seemed it did eventually for all Newfoundlanders, to set out on their journey westward. Alberta was not a place to retire to but a place where people went to start again, to make a new beginning. And that was how they spoke of it.

After wandering for years from house to house all over the Goulds, my mother, when they were finally able to afford a house of their own, had wound up by necessity in one directly across the road from her father's. That, literally and figuratively, it seemed to her, was how far she had got, that was the limit of her life's adventure and her leash, across the road. She had faced south for twenty-five years, then crossed the road to spend the next twenty-five facing north, the view reversed. It was as though she had stood on the same spot all her life and in the middle of her life had merely turned around.

It was years now since the farm had failed. Her father's house was being lived in by strangers, the land behind it unworked in years, growing over with wild grass and hay, alders, juniper and spruce. The old forest that her father cleared was growing back after years of waiting on the borders of the field for him to leave. The outbuildings, all looking as if some bored giant had crumpled them slightly in passing, were windowless, doorless, their roofs caved in. The cellar had all but fallen into the hole it had sheltered for decades. Watching the farm they had all worked so hard to preserve pass slowly into ruin was not how she wanted to spend the balance of her life.

I had left when I was forty years younger than they were now. For the first time, I knew better than they did what they were facing. But it was not something that I could prepare them for. They were setting out like a pair of youngsters who had never been far from home before and were more exhilarated than apprehensive at not knowing what was waiting for them.

I came back from the mainland supposedly to help them move but really because my own leaving had still not taken and I thought that leaving with them, spending the last night with them in the house, would change that and I would at last feel what I ought to have when I left alone twelve years earlier and again eight years after that.

On the night before they left, my parents, my younger sister, Stephanie, and I slept on the floor of the living room in sleeping bags borrowed from Harold and Marg, who would retrieve them after we were gone. My parents insisted that no one go to the airport to see us off.

Their luggage was packed and piled up in the porch. Everything had either been sold or sent west. There were not even curtains on the windows. The car they had rented for the last couple of days and would leave at the airport was in the driveway. Their flight was very early in the morning, just after sunrise. My father, for the first time in forty years, had a purpose for getting up at four and for the first time in forty years would not be getting up alone.

The four of us sat on the living room floor with our backs against the wall, our lower halves in sleeping bags. My parents smoked cigarettes. My father and my sister talked. Their voices echoed in the empty house, which smelled as it had when it was new. The lights of cars passing on Petty Harbour Road lit

up the room every few minutes, moved at first slowly and then
swiftly across the ceiling before vanishing abruptly.

My mother and my sister fell asleep. I could hear them breathing evenly, my mother still sitting with her back against the
wall, my sister slumped beside her.

My father, perhaps thinking I was asleep, got up and went
out to the kitchen. I heard him light a cigarette.

There is a question I want to ask him, the same question I
almost asked him the night before I went away when we stood
at the barrel, staring into the fire, a question that still seems
unthinkable to ask. Back then I thought I could bear to live in
permanent suspense, but for some time now have been feeling
I cannot.

I remember how, on his last ride on the train, my father
shouted at the fact-facing bus-boomer. How can I even think
what I am thinking? That I am even able to consider it, I tell
myself, have been telling myself for years, is a measure of how
things must have been back then. An epidemic of suspicion,
treachery, guilt, paranoia. Why do I so much want to know if
I am right?

I get up, tiptoe across the room and down the hall. I stand
in the doorway of the kitchen. My father is leaning sideways on
the counter in his customary manner, looking out the window.
The kitchen is empty of all furniture and knickknacks, and the
sight of him there savouring in solitude his last night in his house
almost makes me change my mind.

I could leave the question unasked and instead tell him
some things that I doubt anyone but he could understand. That

I have chosen the one profession that makes it impossible for me to live here. That I can only write about this place when I regard it from a distance. That my writing feeds off a home-sickness that I need and that I hope is benign and will never go away, though I know there has to be a limit. And that someday it will break my heart.

I could tell him that I know as well as he does how it feels to crave what you can never have.

That I know his grievous wound was self-inflicted and that leaving will not heal it.

That he will come back to this place that he sometimes thinks he hates, while I who never think of it with anything but love must stay away.

That years ago, when I first left the island, as the ferry pulled away from Port aux Basques, I looked back with near contempt on this place that I believed could not contain me. I was too young to understand that the mainland, the main land, that I believed that I was headed for, did not exist. It existed neither for the people I was soon to meet nor for the people I had left behind, neither for him nor for his father, nor for the castaways and exiles who first wintered on the shores of Newfoundland.

That I am still too young to understand all this, but I know it's true.

Just past him, outside the window, are the steps on which I used to stand and face into the wind when I knew a storm was coming. The east wind that blew in from the Shoal Bay Hills and still smelled of the unseen North Atlantic.

The storms moved from west to east, their clouds, winds, rain or snow from east to west. A simple but maddening para-dox. Like a person walking towards the rear of an airplane.

Everything the storms contained moved two opposing ways at once.

I could tell him that sometimes when I close my eyes and cannot sleep, I see them moving eastward on the weather map, the wind within them blowing back the way they came.

In six hours, the new owners will arrive with their belongings and the space within these walls will be transformed.

On March 31, 1949, he sat by himself in his room at college and kept just such a vigil over Newfoundland as he is keeping now.

"Back in 1948 —" I say.

He turns his head and looks at me.

"Back in 1948," I say again, "in the referendum —"

I pause to give him a chance to interrupt. It is still not too late to withdraw, but he says nothing.

"Did you vote for independence?" I say.

"Yes," he says, not as though he is offended or surprised, but as though he was expecting me to ask, as though it is a perfectly reasonable question, though it seems to me that it would only be so if he answered no.

"I voted for independence," he says, exhaling the sentence like a sigh, as if he is tired of answering this question but resigned to being asked it. "I did," he says, and this time it might be a sigh not of weariness but of relief that at long last he has told someone, unburdened himself.

But what has he told me? Is he admitting to doubts he has secretly entertained since 1948 about whether he chose the right side in the referendum? But surely such doubts would only nag him if the side he voted for had won.

"Was Charlie —"

"He used to tell me things. He never had to ask me to keep them to myself. I told him some things too."

He shakes his head, straightens up from the sink as if to say that he would like the kitchen to himself again.

Charlie. Could that have been what he left out in his account of their parting on the beach?

Charlie. Confessing to his son what he confessed to no one else, his son whom he knew would keep his secret but whom he did not know he would never see again. Charlie unburdening himself, Charlie guilt-ridden, remorseful, realizing too late that he had blundered. Or merely giving in to the urge to share a secret he could no longer stand to keep.

Knowing what I did about him, I could not imagine it. Not Charlie.

Why *not* Charlie? The closet confederates. Apparent zealots to the cause, for whom everyone who knew them would have vouchsafed. As everyone who knew him would have done for Charlie.

But no, not Charlie.

Nan? Might their falling-out have been in some way over her? My father defending her, Charlie...It was just as likely to have been one of his brothers and sisters as Nan. Or someone I had never heard of, someone from my father's life before he met my mother, someone whose politics were at odds with Charlie's. A woman's?

No. It must have been Charlie.

I look at my father. A decision he must have agonized over has been taken. He is leaving Newfoundland tomorrow to start a new life on the Prairies at the age of sixty-four. He does not want to drag up things that might make him reconsider or cause him to leave in a state of mind that will fate this late-life experiment to failure.

"Forget about all that," he says, turning back to the window. "That was all before your time. There's no need for you to get caught up in that."

He is right. There is no point.

Something, some thing, a shift, a swing, a fall took place that would have taken place no matter which side won. There is no point, in his case, trying to remember, or in mine to imagine, how things used to be.

No path leads back from here to there.

We cannot find the way because there is none.

"Try to get some sleep," he says.

WE LEFT THE house under cover of darkness, unseen, as far as we knew, by neighbours, hustled the luggage to the car, whispering as if we were making some sort of getaway and if discovered would be forced to stay. It was still solid night when we took our last look at the house. We could barely make it out. Already it appeared to belong to someone else. My mother did not even try to take a last glance at her father's house, now lived in by people from the city. She could not have seen the farm behind it if she had tried.

We drove into St. John's along the south-side arterial road that was built into the Brow and from which the sunrise view of the old city was so spectacular it was like an admonition. The variously coloured clapboard houses on whose fronts the sun shone as it only ever did at this time of day and time of year seemed illuminated from within, all the different colours tinged with early-morning orange.

The Johnstons, driving in the shadow of the Brow where the street lamps were still burning, could not see the sun, only its light reflected on the houses and on the granite cliff face of the Battery at the foot of Signal Hill. My father had planned to take the newer, north-side arterial and skirt the city altogether. But he had from habit taken the route he had followed to work for thirty years.

We descended into the city, headed east, facing straight into the sun and were blinded by it. At Rawlin's Cross my father turned right instead of left, onto Military Road. We were, as if not meant to make a clean getaway, in the city, so he might as well, he said, do what he had sworn for months he would not do. He drove down Military Road until we reached the old Colonial Building, across from which he parked the car.

It had been the site of the Newfoundland legislature from 1850 to 1960, not the first, which had been a tavern, or the second, which had been an orphanage, but the third. It was now the provincial archives, repository of the past, the past put out to pasture.

My sister was by this time asleep in the back seat. My mother stared straight ahead, praying that my father would not, at this last second, change his mind. My father, the car idling, rolled down his window and stared across the courtyard, at the six Ionic columns and the ten steps that led up to them. "The whole thing was a sham," my father muttered.

"It was forty years ago," my mother said.

I wondered if the question I had asked my father the night before and the one I had almost asked had provoked him into taking this last look. If there had been no one in the car but him and me, if not for my sister and my mother being there, I might have tried again.

My father had not given the Colonial Building this long a look for decades. The ghost history of Newfoundland. The Colonial Building. Cashin as prime minister. The Pink, White

and Green as the national flag. In that ghost history, the independents had won the referendum, the members of the national parliament of Newfoundland had been meeting since 1949,
and it was Joey's and not Cashin's name whom no one under
forty could remember.

My father drove on towards the airport.

The last structure of any size that we passed along the way
was the cathedral-like Confederation Building, set on the highest point of land in the city. Built in 1960, it consisted of a
centre tower that for years had been the tallest building in the
province, and two massive wings on either side. For twelve
years, it had been Joey's secular basilica, from the top floor of
which his west-facing office overlooked the city of St. John's.

There are two runways, from either one of which, depending
on the wind and visibility, a plane bound for the mainland may
take off from the airport at St. John's.

One runway faces almost due west and is the one used
when the prevailing wind is blowing. A plane that uses this
runway does not change direction after takeoff. The other faces
almost due east and is most often used when the wind blows
strong from that direction, as it does just before and during
storms, as it was the morning the Johnstons left — there
was an onshore gale heralding a storm that was still a good
way off.

Our plane took off into the wind and headed out to sea
as if our destination was the Old World. We crossed over

Signal Hill and made a slow turn that brought us even with Cape Spear, the sunshine revolving through the cabin like the light of an accelerated day. The plane banked steeply, then straightened out. We again passed over Signal Hill, again over the airport, gaining altitude, heading west.

Soon we were crossing over a part of Newfoundland more cratered than the moon, round blue ponds that might have been tidal pools, for next we saw and flew over open water.

For a time we flew within sight of the south coast, across the boot of the Burin Peninsula, between the Baie d'Espoir peninsula and the islands of St. Pierre and Miquelon.

"The *Belle Bay* run," I said.

My father nodded. But he was not looking out the window. He was staring at his hands, at his fingers that were so tightly entwined their tips were bright red and the rest of them was bloodless.

And then we were clear of the land altogether and below us there was nothing but the water of the Gulf.

"NINE VOTES FOR Newfoundland!" he shouts as, with his family, he walks into the hall. The referendum is so close it might not be decided until the returns come in from Labrador.

He thinks of Nan the night before, making calculations on a slate to see if their lead on the island was large enough to hold up in spite of Labrador. She has never been to Labrador. She has never travelled more than forty miles from Ferryland, never seen the Isthmus of Avalon except on maps.

Not until he pulls the curtain closed behind him does the possibility occur to him. He looks around, at the chair and the little table, at the makeshift plywood ceiling. Why a voting booth should need a ceiling — the whole thing reminds him of confession.

He cannot help feeling that behind the curtain some priest sits in profile, face resting on his hand, waiting patiently for him to speak. This is even more private than confession.

"Bless me, Father."

In one hand he holds a pencil, in the other a piece of paper on which two boxes have been drawn, an inch apart. It is easy to imagine, looking at the paper and the simple diagram, that the whole matter is his to decide.

"Choose one," the paper reads.

There were no arguments in his house about Confederation, nor, as far as he knew, in any other house in Ferryland.

Elsewhere, lifelong friends were at each other's throat about it. Houses were literally divided, a confederate wife sticking to one half of a house, an independent husband to the other. He has heard of a man who broke off his engagement when his fiancée spoke up for independence. And of a family that each night eats dinner in silence, one half wearing on their pockets or lapels badges that proclaim their position on "the question" or bear brazenly the image of the man the other half regards as the anti-Christ.

He has neither heard nor read the arguments in favour of Confederation except when they were set up as straw men to be knocked down by Independents, and is therefore unable to weigh one side against the other.

A solitary impulse makes him choose.

He does not sit down. He knows he must not linger, they will be suspicious if he does.

He lays the paper on the table and keeps it in place with his left hand while with his right he scrawls an X. He will wonder later if his hand was God guided to do what to him seemed and always will seem wrong, if others were likewise moved to go against what they believed, perhaps more than half as many as the margin of defeat.

His heart, when he leaves the booth, is pounding. His hands shake so badly he has to use both of them to fit the piece of paper in the slot.

As they make their way back home along the road below the Gaze, a man, frantic, embarrassed, runs past them, headed for the parish hall. Someone tells him that should he not make it in time and should independence lose by just one vote, he will be strung up.

The words "one vote" linger in his mind.

He stops and, turning his back to the Gaze, looks out across the Pool. His house, like all the others, faces the sea. His evening prospect, all his life, has been the sea.

He wonders if they have counted his vote yet.

"To reach St. John's from North America," the Major said, "you have to travel a quarter of the way to England. The Azores are closer than Toronto to St. John's. Our island is farther from its mainland than Ceylon or Madagascar are from theirs."

He had no idea where the Azores or any of those other places were except Toronto, which he doubted he would ever see. This was in a church hall in Cape Broyle. He wondered what the Major was getting at.

"We are neither there," the Major said, pointing one way, "nor there," pointing the other.

He stood with his arms outstretched, one pointing east, one pointing west.

"We are *here!*" the Major roared, bringing both hands together palm to palm, then entwining his fingers to make a single, massive fist, which he brought down on the table with such force that people jumped.

He turns in at their laneway with the others and walks up to his house.

He notes from the kitchen window the sudden change in the colour of the water near the shore as the sun sinks below the Gaze, watches the shadow move east across the Pool until, with the real sunset, it moves too fast for him to follow and the light, without his having seen it leave, is gone.

When they lose, when the voice on the radio says that "in our great but troubled history a strange new chapter has begun," he cries like all the others.

"My poor little country, gone," he says.

They do not know. None of them will ever know.

The moon, a sliver, yellow crescent, can be seen above the Gaze.

FOR SIX YEARS they lived abroad. He survived the heart attack he had only a few weeks after leaving Newfoundland. Four years later, one day after returning to Alberta after his first visit back to Newfoundland, he had a stroke.

They came back. Perhaps he had planned to do so all along, hoping that he would return to find the place as profoundly transformed as he had the first time he returned to it in 1949.

I flew home so I could be there to meet them when their plane touched down. When you turn the corner into the short corridor that leads to the terminal at the airport in St. John's, you find yourself face to face with a throng of people gawking eagerly as if they have gathered to welcome home a local hero fresh from some triumph on the mainland.

I have never felt more left out, more self-consciously alone than when I've arrived at that airport with no one there to meet me. I was anxious that my father not feel that way, that there be among that crowd as he turned the corner as many familiar faces as possible.

He came down the tunnel holding my mother's arm, while a flight attendant whose help he swore he did not need walked gingerly beside him. Many other relatives and friends were there, but the sight of me unsettled him. He looked as if he wondered if some stroke-induced forgetfulness had made him lose track of where I lived.

"You're home again," I said.

"Home again," he said, smiling sheepishly as if he had been caught in some bit of foolishness. "You're home again, too."

"I just wanted to see the look on your face," I said. "I'm just here for a few days." We hugged. He seemed to have grown even shorter. I could have rested my chin on his head.

He looked around the small terminal, shaking his head in wonder, disbelief, dismay. Time, this time, had had no effect except on him. The past, neither by his leaving nor his coming back, had been undone.

But he had survived, he had seen through to its conclusion some inscrutable necessity.

HIS COUNTRY AND his father gone, my father came back home in May of 1949, crossing Newfoundland by train from west to east, soon to visit his father's grave for the first time, and soon to see his family, his brothers, his sisters and his mother for the first time since before his father's death.

He rode coach, as he always did, unable to afford a berth, though on this occasion it didn't matter, for there was no chance that he would have slept. There were only a few differences. A sign at the dock in Port aux Basques read "WELCOME TO NEWFOUNDLAND AND LABRADOR, TENTH PROVINCE OF CANADA."

The train itself no longer bore on its boxcars THE NEW-FOUNDLAND RAILWAY, but instead Canadian National Railway or CNR. The stewards, the bursers, the waiters, the conductor, the engineer and fireman all wore the uniform of the new management. The table cloths and napkins and towels and face cloths were monogrammed CNR.

My father travelled with friends who, like him, were returning home from college. Anti-confederates all, they were

getting their first glimpse of the new Newfoundland and glee-
fully observed that "aside from a few letters," it still looked the
same, as if the Confederates had predicted that if they won
every inch of it would be transformed.

Reaching Riverhead Station in St. John's, my father was
met by an uncle with whom he drove the forty miles of unpaved
road along the Southern Shore to Ferryland. It reminded him of
the time he and Charlie brought back the anvil from the foundry
in St. John's. His uncle stopped the car on the road below the
house and helped my father get his suitcase from the trunk.
Then he drove off.

It must have seemed impossible to my father that so much
could have happened in a year, that to go back in time but one
year would have been to go back before they lost the referendum, before he went fishing for the last time, before he left
home, before his father died, before Newfoundland the country
ceased to be, back to when there was still a fire in the forge
and when, after dark in the fall, behind the windows fogged up
from the heat, he saw the fire surge and fade, surge and fade
as his father worked the bellows, back to when it had been
twenty years since his grandfather died and the forge had gone
unlit so long that the chimney bed was cold. How *could* all that
have happened in one year? How could so much have ended and
so much else begun?

There were still hoofprints on the path that led up to the
forge, along which people led their horses by the bridle to have
them shod, prints left there since last fall and persisting because
the ground had not yet thawed.

He was shocked, looking up the hill towards the house, to
see how lifeless the forge looked. It had never looked its age

before, but now it did, the age that the fire within, the ring of the anvil, the smoke and sparks from the chimney and the light at the windows had belied. It looked not only old, but as if it had been in disuse for years.

The only things unchanged were the rusted scrap heap of iron out back, his father's rough stock of iron, for which he and his children had foraged the Shore on weekends, the ancient mound of yellow ash and the flame-shaped streaks of soot on the rust red chimney bricks. The forge, like a piece of cooled, once-molten metal, had achieved its final form.

It seemed to my father, looking about, that all of Ferryland had achieved its final form, been heated, hammered, doused in the tub, tempered in brine and hardened into fact that would endure like rock. He noticed the silence, what had previously been the silence only of night and early morning and of Sunday afternoons. It was mid-week, mid-afternoon and there came from the forge a discordant silence. All of Newfoundland had been resettled in his absence, its destiny as profoundly changed as if it had been floated on a raft across the Gulf.

After seeing his mother and the rest of his family, he walked alone down the road to the Church of the Most Holy Trinity. He stopped to look at an early iceberg that had made its way into the harbour and run aground and turned the whole Pool cloudy green and left a scum of slush on the surface so that now, after high tide, there was a strand of ice along the shore. The base of the iceberg stretched like a pedestal beneath the water, which was a deep blue-green at the sunken edges. Above the water it was faintly like a house except for one spire of ice that was still attached to the rest, though the intervening part was well submerged. Unless it was dynamited, there would

be no capelin in June, and even larger fish like the cod would
keep their distance, so that to catch them fishermen would have
to travel twice as far as usual. But such considerations were
behind him now. He had not come back to Ferryland to live.

He climbed the hill behind the church to the cemetery on
the Gaze. Following his mother's directions, he found his
father's grave, read the headstone, stood beside it. He turned
and faced the water, looked down at the beach where he had
last seen his father alive.

"Be a good boy."

It had rained the night before, and though the wind had
gone round and was now blowing from the west, storm clouds
were still racing overhead. A west wind in Ferryland was offshore, so there was no fog.

My father could see the whole length of the Downs and,
at the end, Ferryland Head and the lighthouse, whose keeper
must have had a busy, sleepless night.

The beacon of the lighthouse, as if the keeper was testing
it, flashed once. And though it was the middle of the day, my
father could see its brief illumination of the water and the land,
a single revolution of super-illuminating light, like the opposite
of an eclipse. Then it was ordinary day again.

He remembered the echo of the hammer on the anvil. He
looked down at the Head and the islands, Bois and Gosse, the
points of land that caused the echo, that sent up between them
and the Gaze the ceaseless din, the sound of the hammer on the
anvil as it travelled back and forth across the water. Before the
echoes from one blow had faded, another one was struck. There
must have been a final blow that ricocheted from hill to hill,
the echoes subsiding like those of a rifle shot.

On referendum night, Charlie could not have been more devastated if his side had just been declared the losers in a winner-take-all war, if it had just surrendered to a regime to exist honourably under which would be impossible and there was therefore nothing left for him to do but shoot himself.

When the last returns from Labrador came in, confirming the anti-confederate defeat, Nan sat beside him and tried to console him at the kitchen table. His upper body was sprawled across it as he cried with his face between his arms, his forehead on the tablecloth.

Just before midnight he went out and fired up the forge. He did not work or even burn anything in the furnace, just kept the fire roaring all night long, piling on the coal, cranking the bellows to sustain that conflagration of protest, impotence and grief. He drank rum and fed the fire, stared into it, stabbed it with a poker, tears and drops of sweat streaking his soot-stained face as he ignored Nan's pleas to come back to the house.

But the next day, word went round in Ferryland that the Major, Peter Cashin, had vowed that despite the outcome of the vote, he would stop Confederation. All of Ferryland had been ready to march to St. John's as soon as Cashin said the word. But no word from Cashin came.

Once it became clear that not even the Major could salvage the cause, many anti-confederates in Ferryland got obliteratingly drunk and stayed that way for days. Charlie went on a binge that lasted for weeks. Never a man to be mistaken for a stoic, Charlie alternated between rage and grief, sitting slumped at his kitchen table while work went undone, fish went uncaught, crops untended, and customers looking to have their horses shod were turned away. Charlie was incredulous that anyone could think that with the referendum lost, there was any point in putting shoes on horses.

Finally Charlie did get down to work. But he pounded away on the anvil more vigorously than usual in the months after the referendum, spoiling more shoes and nails than he had since he apprenticed with his father. The din from the forge was such that Nan wondered if he was doing anything but striking the anvil.

It had been a longer-than-usual cessation of hammering that sent Nan out to the forge, where she found that her husband had as suddenly and inexplicably given out as his legendary anvil had, one second solid, the next shattered as if he had reached some predetermined limit measured out by hammer strokes.

Charlie lay on the floor of the forge, all his tools scattered about him. She was able to tell how long he had been lying by how low the fire had burned down. In the part of the forge reserved for just-finished pieces there was nothing; nor were there any works-in-progress on the floor or in the vat.

My father turned around again and faced the forge and, for an instant, was convinced that since that final blow, no time had passed, that if he looked in through the window he would see his father and it would still not be too late to say goodbye.

WHERE THE FORGE was, there is nothing now. The site is overgrown with scrub. There are horseshoes lying everywhere, in the grass, above ground and below. You have only to dig with your heel to unearth a shoe or a nail or a rusting railway spike. Sod has grown over Charlie's pile of rough stock, which must have sunk some into the ground, for the mound that my father remembers looking up at is just a few feet high.

They believe they have found the site of Baltimore's great but short-lived mansion on the Downs, a mansion that was razed by pirates, Protestants, weather and decay. They are still trying to puzzle out its shape and dimensions.

The Downs have been marked out on a grid with string, and students and professors from the college in St. John's are sifting through the excavation square by square. In each hole, a person crouches, brushing dust from shards of china, piecing together cups and plates, unearthing cutlery that they hope can be restored.

They have yet to find the salt works mentioned in the letter sent to Lord Baltimore from Ferryland by Edward Wynne in 1622. They are sorting out the floor plan, speculating about which room lay where. There is talk that the whole house will be reconstructed exactly as it was, that one day the people of Ferryland will look out their windows and see what people looking out theirs saw four hundred years ago.

There would have been a day when the Welshmen who preceded him and spent years preparing a place for him saw Lord Baltimore's ships from the top of the Gaze, proof that the Old World had persisted in their absence, that all that lay between them and home was a finite stretch of water. Here was Baltimore, making real again things they had stopped believing in, Baltimore who would never see, as they had, Ferryland before the first ship landed, the place before it had a name, who would never, as they had, draw near to an empty shore feeling as if they had gone back to the brink of time, as if time would begin the moment they set foot upon the beach. They had not arrived at the end of a mission of discovery and exploration as Cabot had in 1497, when he made landfall at Cape Bonavista. They had come to stay for good, as absurd and as terrifying as that must have seemed to them as, in the last few minutes of their journey, they regarded Newfoundland. They had neither his illusions nor the prospect of a quick return to England to sustain them.

Baltimore would never know the loneliness and solitude they felt in those first days. But here at last was "his Lordship" on whose behalf they had been toiling for years but whose existence they did not really believe in, so impossible was it to imagine an aristocrat resident in such a place, however fine his house might be. He would stick out among the colonists the way his unoccupied mansion did among their tilts and huts.

WAYNE JOHNSTON

In his ship was as much of home as he had been able to cram into it. His mansion house was ready for him. It was there, incongruously there for him to see as he hove to in sight of Ferryland.

I have often wondered what he thought when he first set eyes on it, if it matched his expectations, if it was everything his governors had promised it would be. Baltimore, his wife and children looking at their new home as they drew near to it. He was fifty-two years old, beyond the life expectancy of even an aristocrat in the early 1600s. In old age, he was starting over in a place he had never set eyes on, a place where habitation by the white man was still an experiment.

In his portrait, which could pass for Shakespeare's, he looks very much like a man of his time. His neck and his shoulders are enclosed in ruffled layers of white lace, the rest of his body in a long black cloak; he has a moustache, a Van Dyke beard and long hair brushed back behind his ears.

There is in his expression the faintly amused disdain for his portraitist and for all those who will look upon his work that is often seen in portraits from that time. He does not look like someone destined to forsake two thousand years of civilization to start his life again in Newfoundland.

Once he moved in, all that was required to complete the illusion that he was still in England was for him to draw the curtains on his windows. The mansion house had been located not with any mind to shelter from the elements or fend off attack by pirates but to show it off to best advantage to Baltimore on his arrival, to the colonists and to anyone from elsewhere who might be sailing by.

When winter came — the worst one since the colony had

been established — he soon realized what a fool he'd been. Though he gave them shelter in his house, ten of his forty subjects died from scurvy or starvation.

A northeast wind, when it gusted, funnelled down the chimneys, put out the meagre fires and swept in icy drafts throughout the great house, which became an infirmary. The time he spent there would come back to him in nightmares for what little remained of his life. Snow drifted down the chimneys, at first melting, then gathering like ashes in the grates until Baltimore was forced to admit that fires were unfeasible and ordered that the flues be closed and the doors and windows boarded up. Until they ran out of oil for their lanterns, it was barely possible to breathe in the mansion house there was so much smoke. After the oil ran out, the house was dark day and night except for the light from the candles that were rationed out. It was not long before the house was like the steerage hold of a ship, all aboard her trying to ride out the winter the way they had the crossing from the Old World to the New. Seasickness was the one affliction they were spared. But there was no pilot to tell them how much progress they were making, how much longer they would be confined or what he thought their chances were. Those few who, in the fever of starvation and disease, ventured out reported snow so deep and ice so thick they were sure they would never melt no matter how long summer, if it ever came, might be.

Everyone in the mansion house was given extreme unction by the priests who had made the crossing with Lord Baltimore. Messages were written informing those who might one day find their remains that they were Catholics and desired to be buried as such. It seemed when the candles were put out that there was nothing in the world but the droning of the wind.

In the spring he took with him back to England all those who survived the winter. He deserted the mansion house, left all its contents and furnishings behind. This is what they are digging up, what lies beneath the town of Ferryland, beneath the site of Charlie's house and what remains of Charlie's forge.

They sailed out of the Pool and, if they looked back, saw the first ghost town of the New World, the mansion house barely finished but deserted on the Downs, forts and wharves and huts made from trees around whose fresh stumps wood chips still lay scattered.

I have often imagined Baltimore and his family standing on the deck of their ship, watching with relief the land recede. Theirs was the first casting-off, the first abandonment, the first admission of defeat. They were the first to pack up and leave everything behind. They blazed a trail of retreat that many after them would follow.

They probably believed that not only Ferryland but all of Newfoundland was uninhabitable and they were taking what for all time would be the last look at the place that anyone would take.

Within a year he made plans to begin a colony on what he had been assured were the more moderate shores of the continent, southeast of Newfoundland, a place called Maryland. The land of Mary after Charles I's queen, to him Mary the Virgin whose likeness in ice would three hundred years later pass within a mile of where he lived. Before he could set sail for his new colony, he died.

BY THE TIME Nan comes back with her two daughters who kneel on the floor beside him, the coals in the forge have reignited and the steam is gone.

Nan clutches his hammer hand in both of hers. The part of her hand between her index finger and her thumb is joined to that part of *his* hand. She squeezes so tightly she does not realize that the pulse she feels is hers.

"Please," she says, "Please." This must have happened because of something she has done. She tells God she is sorry, asks him to forgive her and says that she will make amends if He will let her husband live.

Few people in Ferryland have phones. Few men spend even the worst winter days at home, so there is no quick way of spreading the news, no telling when some man might come knocking at the door to pay Charlie or to find out why his horse has not been shod, so Nan's brother, Will, keeps watch at the bottom of the Gaze and Charlie's brother Mike keeps watch above the forge for men who might stop by for their horses on their way home from the woods.

Uncle Mike is several times obliged to break the news of his brother's death to men he hardly knows.

As word of what has happened at the forge spreads through the town, men come to get their horses and their ponies and lead them by their bridles down the hill. They do not stop to express their condolences to Nan. It is too soon for that. This goes on for hours. From inside the house, they can hear the slow clopping of the horses as one by one they are led away.

By nightfall, one horse is still tethered to the rail, that of a man so shy that for him to meet any of the Johnstons under these circumstances would be unbearable.

Will leads the horse along the road above the beach where shore ice clatters as waves he cannot not see break on the rocks. And though it is only seven o'clock, he finds the man's house unlit, its owner pretending he is out or gone to bed. Will opens the gate, leads the horse into the yard, then walks back to Charlie's house alone.

How, Nan wonders, can so much have changed in just one day? The horses, the sight and sound and smell of them, are gone. There is no din from inside the forge, no condensation on the windows, no reflection from within. The fire has gone out for the first time in twenty years. From now until they tear it down there will be a Sunday silence in the forge.

It does not yet seem to Nan that she has crossed a divide in time. It still seems to her that time has stalled, that there have been a succession of Sundays, and any morning now when she wakes up Monday will have come at last, and Charlie and the horses and every aspect of her life that for the past few months has been on hold will be restored. But from now on, the hill below the forge will be empty in the morning. No one looking out from Charlie's room will see the horses any more.

He LOOKS OUT upon an empty yard as he goes to bed.

When he wakes up he looks out again and sees waiting patiently for him horses who seem to have gathered of their own accord while he was sleeping. In the hope of beating others to it, of having them shod in time to use them later that same day for hauling wood, the first men led their horses up the hill and tied them to the rail at three o'clock. Charlie and Nan, accustomed to the sound of horses going past outside the window, slept through it.

It is still dark as, for the last time, he looks out his bedroom window and sees the horses waiting for him on the hill below the forge, standing chest-deep in the morning mist that when he steps outdoors an hour later will be gone.

How many horses are there? Twenty, thirty, forty? He is too tired to count them. Today, as always, there are too many.

Somewhere among them is the last horse he will shoe today. Her name is Nancy. After Nancy, instead of going to the rail to get another horse, he will go to the forge, where Nan will find him sometime later.

Some of these horses were culled from wild herds descended from other herds who first ran free two hundred years ago, horses that were abandoned by or escaped from settlers, or after battles went unclaimed or were impossible to catch, herds that, during winter cold spells, still come down from the Gaze at night and roam the road and lanes in search of food.

He sees the usual descending series of variously coloured manes and rumps along the rail. Frost snorts from their noses as though a line of infantry is firing at will. He wonders how long it will take to shoe them all.

Fishing season is over, so he can get an early start, but he doubts that he will have them done by dark. There is no time for breakfast. Nan will bring him something later — toutons, fried bread dough slick with butter. He will go on working, a touton in his mouth as he holds a horse's hoof between his knees.

In the porch, the drinking water in the wooden pails has frozen solid. He brings one pail indoors for Nan and takes the other two with him to the forge. If yesterday was anything to go by, he will need at least two buckets, maybe more. He puts them against the brick bed, empties a scuttle of coal on top, then inserts the bellows in the space between the bricks. He works the bellows with his hands and feet.

Inside the tub of brick, unseen by him though he can smell it, the fire that has not burned out for years starts to make its way towards the surface, until at last the coals on top begin to smoke and finally ignite to an orange crust of embers. Throughout the day, to keep this crust from cooling, to keep the ash from going grey, he will have to work the bellows twice an hour, maybe more.

The countdown on the old black slate continues. Each day has its number. Today's is 76. Seventy-six days left until Confederation.

He cannot imagine writing single digits on that slate ten weeks from now, much less erasing from the slate the number '1.'

He heard the other day that on referendum night, in every independent riding, there were still people lined up waiting when the polling booths were closed. But in the confederate ridings, the voting went like clockwork.

Every day, there is some new revelation of this sort. He cannot allow himself to think about it. He must think of something else or soon the rum he has hidden on the shelf above the slack tub will be in his hand and his work will go undone.

He thinks of Art in Nova Scotia, barely old enough to vote. They have had no letters from him. Boys from Ferryland have gone away to school and not been heard from since. He told Art it was worse to say goodbye at sunset than not to say goodbye at all. "That's just superstition," his son said, as if he was going away to purge himself of things like superstition. He told him if he waited until morning he would drive him to St. John's. "And in the morning," his son said, "there'll be some other reason not to go."

He does the easy horses first. A pony that meekly submits to being shod, a mare so used to this routine she needs no bridle but when he unties her merely walks behind him as he plods up to the forge. He knows these horses better than he knows their owners. These horses who are oblivious to circumstance, neither more nor less content than they were six months ago. He is tired of telling himself he ought to learn from their example.

And then it starts up in his throat as it has every day about this time since Christmas, a scorching pain that nothing but the water in the bucket can put out. When the pain first started, he drank the water from an iron ladle, dipping it time after time into the bucket. Today, he will drink directly from the bucket, drink it dry, tip it back and let the water that began the day as ice pour down his throat.

He is grateful to this pain that has made the water taste as sweet as it did when he was just a boy. As he gulps the water from the wooden bucket, it runs down his chin, then down his neck. He feels the water on his throat, inside and out.

The pain is not gone when he stops drinking. It has been two weeks since it went away completely. The lump of coal lodged in his throat is dowsed but inside it there still burns a core of flame.

He will go to the priest tomorrow and have him bless his throat with a pair of crossed candles the way the old priest did when he was nine. He remembers the priest making a scissors-like X with the candles held flat in front of him, then pushing the crook of the X against his throat as he knelt at the communion rail, the candles cool against his skin, the smell of the wax, the priest pushing them against his Adam's apple with increasing force until he was barely able to suppress the urge to cough.

It is said that there is still water from the Virgin Berg in barrels in the basement of the church. Perhaps the priest might prescribe some if he asked, one healing ladleful or even teaspoonful a day until the pain is gone. He thinks of the water cooling in those casks for forty years.

He has drunk the better part of a bucket of water, but he does not feel full. He does not feel anything except that ember in his throat. It seems to him there is no amount of water that he could not drink, no receptacle he could not drain dry and still be thirsty.

He raises the second bucket of water to his lips. It is just like the other but is suddenly so heavy that he can barely lift it. His hands, his whole arms tremble.

The bucket, when he falls, strikes the brick edge of the bed, teeters there, then topples over, the water spilling out across the coals from which rises a cloud of steam so thick it fills the forge. He does not hear the hiss as the water, evaporating as it goes, seeps down between the coals.

He knows that he is lying on the cold floor of the forge, flat on his back. Someone, a man he thinks, comes towards him from the mist, stands over him and looks down at him but does not speak. He thinks this man must be a fetch, the apparition of someone not long dead or soon to die.

He thinks at first it must be the Major who has died.

He recalls what Bedivere asked Arthur. "What shall become of me, now ye go from me, and leave me here alone among mine enemies?"

"Comfort yourself," King Arthur said, "and do the best you can. But trust no more in me."

No. It is not Cashin. Not the Major. Nan? No. One of his sons. It might be Art. The farther from home someone is, the more likely you are to see their fetch. A well-known fact. The man goes back into the mist.

He sees three women in the mist and now he knows it must be Art, his second son. He remembers someone telling him what "*morte d'Arthur*" meant, but he called him Arthur anyway, for he loved the story, and King Arthur when he died was very old.

What can have happened to his son who is only twenty-three? Just a boy.

"Be a good boy."

And then Art turned away, without a word. He cannot remember why. He climbed the beach rocks to the road and got into the car without a wave.

Someone is kneeling at his side and begging his forgiveness.

"Please, please —"

He feels his hammer hand enclosed by someone whose grip is so much stronger than his own that his hand goes limp.

Not Nan. Not Arthur. Then who? No one. He must have paused to rest and nodded off, and in what his father called a dwall have had a dream. A misunderstanding, nothing more.

He has never felt such peace. He cries. Tears run down his temples. He would wipe them with his hands if he could move. No one has been taken from him. He will see them all again. Sleeping on the job. What would the Major think? In a moment he will rouse himself and get back to work. But for now he will linger in this slumber.

When he wakes from the dwall, he is standing at the window of the forge. The mist has begun to lift, but the channel between the islands and Hare's Ears through which the man aimed the camera at the Virgin Berg when he was twelve is still obscured by fog.

If the Virgin had arrived on such a day, she would have sailed on past the island unseen by anyone. Or seen only by fishermen so close to her they could not make out her shape. He and his father in their boat might have bumped up against her and not known it.

He hears from somewhere deep inside the fog a woman's voice, a woman whispering, and then another's, and possibly a third and fourth, four women conversing in some urgency as if together they are piloting their craft to shore, listening for the sound of water breaking on obstacles they cannot see, reefs and rocks, jutting fingers of the coast, trying to ply a safe passage to a shore whose distance from them they ought to be able to remember but cannot.

He has many times made his way into the Pool in just this fashion; he knows what they are going through. He has many times waited on the beach like this for the landing of a boat, knowing it was best that he not call out, for in the fog it would only confuse the unseen navigators.

He waits, as he so often has, to hear their boat's bell and to see the light from the lantern held aloft by someone standing in the prow, peering, squinting to distinguish phantom shapes from real ones.

As the fog begins to lift and he can see more and more water, the voices of the women grow louder and Charlie is certain that he will see them soon.

He thinks he faintly hears the plash of oars, every few seconds, the long, slow gentle stroke of some reluctant rower whose back is to the shore, who must look over her shoulder to see and take direction from the woman standing in the prow. Their voices, speaking words that he cannot make out, grow louder still and it seems to him he should have seen their boat by now.

The voices are closer than the fog, which has retreated even further, a woman's voice and the voices of girls — he cannot tell how many.

He hears his name spoken playfully, tenderly, by a woman whose lips he would swear are at his ear. The voices pass over him, around him, through him, and the unseen woman and her girls go up the hill towards the Gaze, laughing, happy to be home.

He turns around.

He cannot even hear them now.

Light pours in through the windows of the forge, which faces east, so it must be morning.

Somehow he has slept all night. No one has thought to look for him in this most obvious of places.

He goes outside. There are no horses, no hoofprints in the ground. He walks down the Gaze, crosses the road, then goes down to the beach, where at the water's edge he stands, looking out to sea. He waits.

He hears the clatter of the rocks on the beach behind him. Someone is coming, someone he knew would meet him here if he waited long enough. But when he looks behind him, there is no one.

The last blow of the hammer on the anvil still echoes back and forth between Hare's Ears and the Gaze as Charlie steps into the fog. He can hear Nan calling to him from outside the fog, but from which side he cannot tell, shouting his name over and over as if she is lost. "Charlie. Charlie." He tells her not to move. He will soon have a fix on where she is.

Someone not Nan speaks.

By the time Nan finds his body on the floor of the forge, he is back on the beach and the fog has lifted. Something happened on this patch of beach, but he cannot remember what. As he looks out at the sea, everything is as it was before he crossed the stream, before he crossed over into Avalon.

The House, the Gaze, the Beach, the Downs, the Pool, Ferryland Head, Hare's Ears, Bois Island, Gosse Island and the sea.

All are fixed in a moment that for him will never pass.

Acknowledgments

Thank you to my peerless editor and friend at Knopf Canada, Diane Martin; to Louise Dennys, my publisher; to Sharon Klein, my heavenly publicist; and to my agent, Anne McDermid.

Wayne Johnston's latest novel (his fifth), *The Colony of Unrequited Dreams*, has been published internationally to tremendous critical acclaim. The film version of a previous novel, *The Divine Ryans*, was released in 1999. *Baltimore's Mansion* was the recipient of the inaugural Charles Taylor Prize for Literary Non-Fiction. Wayne Johnston was born and raised in Newfoundland and now lives in Toronto.